DAD JOKES

THE PUNNIEST JOKE BOOK EVER

WARNING: Contents may lead to eye rolling, cringing, and groaning OR sidesplitting, knee-slapping, gut-busting laughter. Probably both!

Portable Press
An imprint of Printers Row Publishing Group
10350 Barnes Canyon Road, Suite 100, San Diego, CA 92121
www.portablepress.com • e-mail: mail@portablepress.com

Publisher: Peter Norton
Associate Publisher: Ana Parker
Publishing/Editorial Team: Vicki Jaeger, Tanja Fijalkowski, Lauren Taniguchi
Editorial Team: JoAnn Padgett, Melinda Allman, Dan Mansfield
Production Team: Jonathan Lopes, Rusty von Dyl

Edited by J. Carroll
Interior design by Susan Engbring
Content curated by Brian Boone and Tanja Fijalkowski
Cover design by Michael Sherman

Library of Congress Cataloging-in-Publication Data

Title: Dad jokes : the punniest joke book ever.
Description: San Diego : Portable Press, 2017.
Identifiers: LCCN 2017001669 | ISBN 9781626861770 (paperback)
Subjects: LCSH: Fathers--Humor. | Fatherhood--Humor. | BISAC: HUMOR / Form / Jokes & Riddles. | FAMILY & RELATIONSHIPS / Parenting / Fatherhood.
Classification: LCC PN6231.F37 D325 2017 | DDC 818/.602--dc23
LC record available at https://lccn.loc.gov/2017001669

Printed in the United States of America

22 21 20 19 18   3 4 5 6 7

CONTENTS

THE DAILY GRIND
Work, School, and Other Necessary Evils

Q: What do you call a person who is happy on a Monday?
A: Retired!

I used to work at a calendar factory, but I got fired for taking a couple days off.

Q: What does Dr. Jekyll do first thing every morning?
A: He wakes up.

There was a robbery at the Apple Store today. They caught the guy because they had an iWitness.

"Sergeant! Sergeant! The troops are revolting!"
"Well, you're no prize pig yourself."

Q: What does a dentist get on his one-year work anniversary?
A: A little plaque.

Rusty shows up late for work. The boss approaches him as he walks in.

"You should've been here at 8:30!" he yells.

Rusty looks surprised. "Why? What happened at 8:30?"

Did you know that name-dropping at work is the worst thing you can do? My coworker Robert De Niro told me that.

Knock-knock!
Who's there?
Highway cop.
Highway cop who?
Highway cop in the morning and
have a cup of coffee.

Did I ever tell you I had a job smashing cans?
It was soda pressing.

Q: How is Christmas like another day at the office?

A: Because you do all the work and some fat guy in a suit gets all the credit!

A lady was expecting the plumber at ten o'clock. Ten o'clock came and went; no plumber. Eleven o'clock, twelve o'clock, even one o'clock rolled around, still no plumber. She concluded he wasn't coming, and left to do some errands.

While she was out, the plumber knocked on the door. Her parrot, which was in a cage by the door, said, "Who is it?"

"It's the plumber."

He thought it was the lady who had said, "Who is it?" and waited for her to let him in. When this didn't happen, he knocked again, and again the parrot said, "Who is it?"

"It's the plumber!"

Still no one answered the door. He pounded on the door, and the parrot repeated, "Who is it?"

"It's the plumber!" he said, irritated.

Again, he waited; again, she didn't come;

again, he pounded; again, the parrot said, "Who is it?"

"AHHHH!" he said, flying into a rage. He kicked the door in. He suffered a heart attack and fell dead in the doorway.

The lady came home from her errands, only to see the door ripped off its hinges and a corpse lying in the doorway. "A dead body!" she exclaimed. "Who is it?"

"It's the plumber!" the parrot answered.

Q: Why do barbers make good drivers?
A: They know all the shortcuts.

At a meeting, the corporate manager told a joke. Everyone on the team laughed except for one guy.

"Didn't you understand my joke?" the manager asked him.

"Oh, I understood it, but I resigned yesterday."

Q: Why couldn't the lifeguard save the hippie?
A: He was too far out, man.

Want to hear a construction joke?
I'm still working on it.

An archaeologist is the best husband
a woman can have: the older she gets,
the more interested he is in her.

How many politicians does
it take to change a lightbulb?
Two: one to change it and
another one to change it
back again.

Q: What kind of shoes do spies wear?
A: Sneakers.

Quarrier: That's a big rock!
Foreman: Boulder.
Quarrier: WOW, WOW, WOW! YOU HAVE
TO LOOK AT THAT ENORMOUS ROCK
OVER THERE!

I went to the bank and asked the teller to check my balance.
    She shoved me, but I didn't fall down.

Q: How did the farmer mend the holes in his jeans?
A: With cabbage patches.

I call my toilet "the jim" instead of "the john." That way I can tell people that I go to the jim first thing every morning.

Newscaster: Why did you relocate across the country?
Weatherman: Because the weather didn't agree with me.

Q: What's the difference between a teacher and a train?
A: A teacher says "Spit out your gum," and the train says "Choo choo choo!"

Every morning I plan on making pancakes,
but I keep waffling.

Q: Why does a queen carry a scepter?
A: Because everyone works 'cept her!

Negotiations between union members and
their employer were at an impasse. The
union denied that workers were flagrantly
abusing their contract's sick-leave provisions.
One morning at the bargaining table,
the company's chief negotiator held up
the newspaper.

"This man," he announced, "called in
sick yesterday!"

There on the sports page was a photo of
the supposedly ill employee, who had just
won a local golf tournament with an excellent
score. A union negotiator broke the silence in
the room.

"Incredible," he said. "Just think of
what score he could've had if he hadn't
been sick!"

Q: What did the ground say to the oil worker?
A: "You bore me."

A magician was driving down the street.
Then he turned into a driveway.

I don't mind going to work every day—
it's the sitting around for eight hours
waiting to go home I can't stand.

Q: Why was the mouse scared of becoming a doctor?
A: He knew he'd have to take the MCAT.

A guy goes into a butcher shop and bets the butcher $50 that he couldn't reach the meat on the top shelf. "No way," said the butcher. "The steaks are too high."

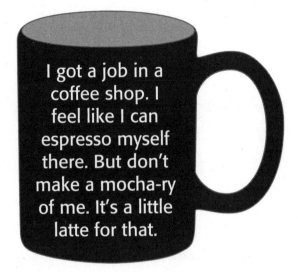

I got a job in a coffee shop. I feel like I can espresso myself there. But don't make a mocha-ry of me. It's a little latte for that.

A police officer jumps into his squad car and radios the station.

"I have an interesting case here," he says. "A woman shot her husband for stepping on the floor she just mopped."

"Have you arrested her?" asks the sergeant.

"No, not yet. The floor's still wet."

Q: What did the tree do when the bank was closed?
A: It started its own branch.

Did you hear about the shipload of paint that wrecked and marooned all the sailors?

Q: What's another name for an eyedropper?
A: A clumsy ophthalmologist.

@gerryhallcomedy

A girl named Ruth quit working at our office. I've been referring to the office as "ruthless" since then.

Customer: Why is this coffee so muddy?
Waitress: It was ground yesterday.

A judge reprimanded a defendant in trial.

"I thought I told you I didn't ever want to see you in my courtroom ever again!" he said.

"I know!" said the defendant. "That's exactly what I tried to tell the police! But they just wouldn't listen to me!"

Q: What do you call an erratic photographer?
A: A loose Canon!

One day while he was building a barn, a cowboy lost his favorite book. A week later, one of his horses came up to him holding the book in its mouth. The cowboy was stunned. He took the book from the horse and said, "It's a miracle!"

"Not exactly," said the horse. "Your name is written inside."

Q: What sound does a bouncing plane make?
A: *Boeing Boeing Boeing…*

A taxi passenger tapped the driver on the shoulder to ask him a question. The driver screamed, lost control of the car, nearly hit a bus, drove up onto the sidewalk, and screeched to a halt just inches from a shop window. For a second everything went quiet in the cab. Then the driver said, "Look, don't ever do that again. You scared the daylights out of me!"

The passenger apologized. "I didn't realize that a little tap would scare you so much."

"Sorry," the driver replied. "It's not really your fault. Today is my first day as a taxi driver. I've been driving a hearse for the last 25 years."

Interviewer: We're looking for someone who is responsible. Do you fit that criteria?
Candidate: Well, in my last job when the store caught fire, my boss said that I was responsible.

I buy my guns from a guy who calls himself
"T-Rex."
  He's a small arms dealer.

Q: Why did the coffee file a police report?
A: It got mugged.

I'm considering getting a job cleaning mirrors.
  It's something I can see myself doing.

Q: Why did the archaeologist have a breakdown?
A: His career was in ruins.

Q: What do you call a police officer who
  refuses to get out of bed?
A: An undercover cop.

To all the coworkers who have talked about
me behind my back: You discussed me.

My friend was fired from a road construction job for theft.

I didn't believe it, but when I went over to his house, all the signs were there.

A bunny hops into a bakery. He asks the baker, "Do you have carrot cake?" The baker says no.

The next day, the bunny returns. He again asks, "Do you have carrot cake?" The baker says no, and again, the bunny leaves.

He returns on the third day. He asks, "Do you have carrot cake?" The baker says no.

That night, the baker thinks about the bunny, and she decides to make a carrot cake. The following morning, as expected, the bunny arrives. He asks the baker, "Do you have carrot cake?"

The baker says enthusiastically, "Yes, I do! I made one last night."

The bunny wiggles his nose and replies, "Gross. No one likes carrot cake."

Did you hear about the lazy baker who asked for a pay increase?
  He really kneaded the dough.

———————

My friend's bakery burned down last night.
His business is toast.

———————

The local caricature artist got arrested. He did always seem sketchy.

———————

Q: Why did the mortgage broker go out of business?
A: He lost interest.

———————

A captain harpooned a whale's tail on his first throw. He said, "Well, that was a fluke."

———————

Q: What do you call a group of security guards in front of the Samsung store?
A: Guardians of the Galaxy.

———————

I heard the new auto body shop in the neighborhood comes highly wreck-amended.

Q: Why was the DJ banned from the supermarket?
A: He was stealing all the samples.

Did you hear about the guy who invented Altoids? He made a mint.

@ceejoyner

Our boss just banned overly specific nicknames and the whole office is staring at Rat Snitch Brian The Good Time Ruiner.

Q: What do you call a fat psychic?
A: A four-chin teller.

I won an award for being the best scarecrow in my field. I told them, "Hay, it's in my jeans."

Q: Where does a general keep his armies?
A: In his sleevies!

My tailor is happy to make a pair of pants for me. At least, sew it seams.

I quit my job as a personal trainer because I'm not big or strong enough. Today, I put in my too-weak notice.

"I can see for miles," said Mile's guide dog.

Q: What did the worker at the rubber band factory say when he lost his job?
A: "Oh, snap!"

A piece of bread attended school. It did so well it made the honor roll.

Q: Why did the elephant leave the circus?
A: He was tired of working for peanuts.

*"Monday is an awful way to spend
1/7 of your life."*

—Steven Wright

The workweek is so rough that after Monday
and Tuesday even the calendar says WTF.

Knock-knock!
Who's there?
Hugh Cosmo.
Hugh Cosmo who?
Hugh Cosmo trouble at work
than anyone else I know!

Knock-knock!
Who's there?
Duet.
Duet who?
Duet right or don't duet at all.

Did you hear about the new dating site for retired chemists?
    It's called "Carbon Dating."

@JermHimselfish

I bet when kittens go to work in kitten offices that there's always one kitten whose cubicle is decorated with pictures of lonely old ladies

---

Q: When's the best time to go to the dentist?
A: Tooth-hurty.

Q: Why did the dentist stick some X-rays in his mouth?
A: Because they were tooth-pics.

Did you hear about the dumb guy who got fired from his job at the M&M's factory?
He kept throwing away all the candies that had W's on them.

Three candies you'll find in every school:
Nerds, DumDums, and Smarties.
One you'll hear in any classroom: Snickers.

Student: Why are we dissecting mushrooms?
Teacher: Because studying fungus is a cultured way to mold young minds.

Q: What's the worst thing about ancient history class?
A: The teachers always Babylon.

Yesterday a clown held the door open for me.
Such a nice jester!

There was a big fire down at the circus.
It was in tents.

Q: Why did the scientist go to the
tanning salon?
A: Because he was a paleontologist.

Knock-knock!
Who's there?
Bumblebee.
Bumblebee who?
Your bumblebee cold if you don't wear pants.

Two atoms were walking down the street.
One turns to the other and says, "Oh, no! I
think I'm an ion!"
  The other asks, "Are you sure?"
  "Yes, I'm positive!"

If I had a dime every time I didn't know what
was going on, I'd be like, "Why is everyone
giving me all these dimes?"

Nothing ruins a Friday quite like
remembering it's actually Tuesday.

Q: How does the Moon cut his hair when the
Sun gets in the way?
A: Eclipse it.

A boss is interviewing a candidate for a job.
The boss asks him, "What do you think is your
worst quality?"

"I'm probably too honest," the man replies.

"That's not a bad thing. I think being honest
is a good quality."

"Good," the candidate answered, "because I
don't care about what you think!"

My last annual performance review said I
 lacked passion and intensity.
They've never seen
me alone with a really
big cheeseburger.

I have some jokes about unemployed people, but none of them work.

Anna gave up her seat to a blind person on the bus.
  That's how she lost her job as a bus driver.

Did you hear about the kidnapping at the school?
  It turned out okay. They woke him up.

Q: What did the nuclear physicist have for lunch?
A: Fission chips.

When I got to work this morning, my boss stormed up to me and said, "You missed work yesterday, didn't you?"
  I said, "No, not particularly."

An employee goes to see his supervisor in the front office. "Boss," he says, "we're doing some heavy housecleaning at home tomorrow, and my wife needs me to help with the attic and the garage, moving and hauling stuff."

"Sorry, but we're shorthanded," the boss replies. "I can't give you the day off."

"Thanks, boss," says the employee. "I knew I could count on you!"

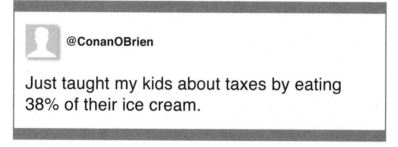

@ConanOBrien

Just taught my kids about taxes by eating 38% of their ice cream.

I don't really work well under pressure. Or under any other circumstance for that matter.

Q: What word is always spelled wrong in the dictionary?
A: Wrong.

Q: What rhymes with orange?
A: No, it doesn't.

I'm not having much luck with jobs lately: I wasn't suited to be a tailor. The muffler factory was just exhausting. I couldn't cut it as a barber. I didn't have the patience to be a doctor. I wasn't a good fit in the shoe factory even though I put my soul into it. The paper shop folded. Pool maintenance was too draining. I got fired from the cannon factory. And I just couldn't see any future as a historian.

An employee was getting to know her new coworkers when the topic of her previous job came up.

"So why did you leave?" asked one coworker.

"It was something my boss said," the new hire replied.

"Why? What did he say?" the coworker asked.

"You're fired."

_____

If Iron Man and the Silver Surfer teamed up, would they be allies...or alloys?

_____

Q: What does Clark Kent use to keep the sun out of his eyes?
A: A supervisor.

_____

Q: What's the difference between a hippo and a Zippo?
A: One's really heavy. The other is just a little lighter.

Sam walks into his boss's office. "Sir, I'll be straight with you. I know the economy isn't great, but I have three companies after me, and I would like to respectfully ask for a raise."

After a few minutes of haggling the boss agrees to a 5 percent raise, and Sam happily gets up to leave.

"By the way," asks the boss, "which three companies are after you?"

"The electric company, the water company, and the phone company," says Sam.

@InternetHippo

"I want to hate my life in a different building"
— person looking for a new job

Q: Where does seaweed look to find a job?
A: In the "Kelp Wanted" section.

The owner of a company told his employees, "You worked very hard this year, and the company's profits increased dramatically. As a reward, I'm giving everyone a check for $5,000!"

Thrilled, the employees gathered round and high-fived one another.

"And if you work this hard next year," the boss continued, "I'll sign those checks!"

Reporter: How do you motivate your employees to be so punctual? **Company owner:** It's simple. I have 100 employees, and 99 free parking spaces outside. The other one costs $50 a day.

A man went to a job interview. His résumé was fantastic, and his qualities made him a perfect fit for the company. The interviewers were very impressed.

"You're a strong candidate, and we would like to hire you. However, there's this five-year gap in your résumé. What were you doing during that time?"

"I went to Yale."

"Wow, great! You're hired!"

"Yay, I got a yob!"

———

Q: Who is the patron saint of e-mail?
A: St. Francis of a CC.

———

Q: How do Buddhist monks send e-mails?
A: They remove all attachments.

———

My greatest professional ambition is to get to a desk where no one can see my computer monitor but me.

A man went to apply for a job. After filling out his application, he waited anxiously while the manager read it. Then the manager said, "We have an opening for people like you."

"Oh, great," the man said. "What is it?"

"The door!"

Q: What did the farmer say when he couldn't find his tractor?

A: "Where's my tractor?"

A mechanic called one of his customers after a check bounced. "The check you wrote to pay your bill came back!" he yelled.

The customer replied, "Well, so did all my car problems that you supposedly fixed!"

People always say that hard work never killed anybody. Oh yeah? When's the last time you've ever heard of anyone who rested to death?

A man was walking down the street and saw a sign in a store window that said "Help Wanted."

He ran in the store and yelled, "What's wrong?"

Q: In an emergency, what's better than an EMT?

A: A pair-a-medics!

@omgthatspunny

If you take a laptop computer for a run you could jog your memory.

An applicant was filling out a job application. When he came to the question "Have you ever been arrested?" he answered no. The next question, intended for people who had answered yes to the previous one, was "Why?" The applicant answered, "Because I never got caught."

June's Boss: Have a good day.
June: Thanks! I'll go home!

_____

A couple of research scientists had twins. They named one John and the other Control.

_____

To surprise her husband, an executive's wife stopped by his office. When she opened the door, she found him with his secretary sitting in his lap. Without hesitating, he dictated, "And in conclusion, gentlemen, budget cuts or no budget cuts, I cannot continue to operate this office with just one chair."

_____

A visitor to a farm asked the farmer, "Why does that one pig have a wooden leg?"

"That pig is the bravest pig I ever saw," the farmer replied.

"So why does he have a wooden leg?" the tourist asked.

"One night, our house caught on fire, and he came inside and woke us all up."

"So…why does that pig have a wooden leg?"

"You can't eat a pig that brave all at once!"

_____

It was mealtime on a small airline, and the flight attendant asked a passenger if he would like dinner.

"What are my choices?" he asked.

"Yes or no."

```
Hey, dad im
sorry but im
dropping out
of school
------------
That's ok,
son, just
remember one
thing
------------
Whats that?
------------
I don't like
pickles on my
Big Mac
```

"Why did you quit your job as an origami teacher?"
"Too much paperwork."

A guy walks into a lawyer's office and asks, "Hey, how much do you charge?"
"I charge $2,500 for three questions."
"Really? That's a bit steep, don't you think?"
"This was great. I accept checks and credit cards."

***

Q: What did the lawyer name his daughter?
A: Sue.

***

Lawyers practice law because it gives them a grand and glorious feeling. You give them a grand and they feel glorious.

—Milton Berle

***

How many editors does it take to change a light bulb?
That was supposed to be in place a week ago!

Q: Why was it called the Dark Ages?
A: Because there were so many knights.

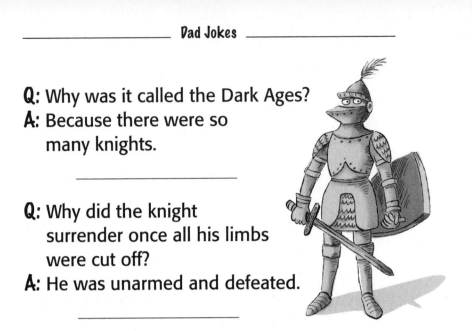

Q: Why did the knight surrender once all his limbs were cut off?
A: He was unarmed and defeated.

An Englishman, a Frenchman, a Spaniard, and a German are all watching an American street performer do some juggling. The juggler notices that the four gentlemen have a very poor view, so he stands up on a wooden crate and calls out, "Can you all see me now?"
"Yes."
"Oui."
"Sí."
"Ja."

Q: What do you call four bullfighters standing in a quicksand pit?
A: Quatro Sinko.

The mad scientist made a clone of himself, but something went wrong—all the clone wanted to do was stick his head out the third-story window and shout dirty words at passersby. The scientist, seeing no other option, pushed the clone out the window. He was arrested for making an obscene clone fall.

@Zaius13

The most embarrassing part about farting myself awake was that it was the most interesting aspect of my PowerPoint presentation.

Q: Why did the orange juice factory worker lose his job?
A: He couldn't concentrate.

A bus stops at a bus station. A train stops at a train station. Now you know why they call it a workstation.

One day an auto mechanic was working under a car and some brake fluid dripped into his mouth. "Wow," he thought. "That stuff tastes good!"

The next day he told a friend about his amazing discovery. "I think I'll have a little more today." His friend was concerned but didn't say anything.

The next day the mechanic drank a whole bottle of brake fluid. A few days later he was up to several bottles a day. And now his friend was really worried.

"Don't you know brake fluid is toxic?" said the friend. "You'd better stop drinking it."

"Hey, no problem," he said. "It's easy for me to stop."

A photon checks into a hotel, and the bellhop says, "Can I get your bags for you?"

"No need, good sir," replies the photon. "I'm traveling light."

I work for the world's biggest nanotechnology company. We're not very good.

So, I asked the dude next to me if he knew the chemical symbol for sodium hypobromite, and he was all like, "NaBrO."

———

"HeHe," said the first chemist.
   "What's so funny?" asked the other.
   "Nothing. I just combined two isotopes of helium."

@arb

ways to get in touch with me, ranked:
1.   text
2.   facebookchat
3.   tweet
4.   email
...
998. skywriting
999. smoke signals
1000. voicemail

Q: What is the biggest difference between chemistry and cooking?
A: In chemistry, you should never lick the spoon.

An aspiring veterinarian put himself through veterinary school working nights as a taxidermist. When he graduated, he decided he could combine the two occupations. On the door of his new business: "Dr. Boone, Veterinary Medicine and Taxidermy: Either way, you get your dog back!"

My book on reverse psychology was just published. Don't read it!

@Sarcasticsapien

[walks up to coworker's desk]
I know I don't say this often enough, but thank you for not showing me pictures of your kids.

Knock-knock!
Who's there?
Cheetahs.
Cheetahs who?
Cheetahs never win
and winners never cheat.

Q: What did the static say to the other static?
A: "I'm sick and tired of your interference!"

A man was flying home from a business trip when the flight attendant handed out brownies. He decided to save them for later, and he put them in the cleanest thing he could find—an unused vomit bag. After the plane landed, the man got up to leave and a flight attendant approached him.

"Sir, would you like me to dispose of that for you?"

"No thanks," he said. "I'm saving it for my kids."

Q: Why can't you trust atoms?
A: They make up *everything*.

Doing a good job at work is like wetting your pants in a dark suit. You get a warm feeling, but no one else notices.

Back in the Wild West, three cowboys were about to be hanged for stealing cattle. The lynch mob brought them to the bank of a nearby river and planned to string them up from a branch over the water. That way, when the men died, they'd just drop into the river and float away.

The mob put the noose around the first cowboy's neck, but he was so sweaty that he slipped right out, fell into the water, and swam away. When the mob strung up the second cowboy, he also slipped out of the noose and got away. As they pulled the third man toward the noose, he hesitated and asked, "Hey, would you tighten that noose? I can't swim!"

A man heard about the discovery of gold in California. He immediately packed up his possessions and moved out west. Six months later, he gave up and returned home. Why? It didn't pan out.

A three-legged dog walks into a saloon in the Old West. He slides up to the bar and announces, "I'm looking for the man who shot my paw."

A rough and tough cowboy had just finished his drink in a tavern. He stood up and walked outside, but a few seconds later he barreled back through the door.

With a mean look on his face and anger in his eyes, he said, "I'm gonna sit back down and have me another drink, and if my horse ain't back where I left it by the time I'm done, I'm gonna have to do what I did back in Texas. And I *really* don't wanna have to do what I done back in Texas!"

He sat back down, finished his second drink, and walked back outside.

Sure enough, his horse was tied back to its post, just where he left it. But right before he departed, one of the scared patrons stopped him and timidly asked,

"Mister, what was it that you had to do back in Texas?"

The cowboy looked him straight in the eye and said:

"I had to walk home."

_____

A rancher was taking inventory of his livestock. He figured that it wouldn't take him too long because he knew for a fact that he had exactly 196 head of cattle. But then he discovered that he actually had 200 head. How'd he do that? He rounded them up.

_____

Q: What happens when the smog lifts off of Los Angeles?
A: UCLA.

Once you've seen one shopping center, you've seen a mall.

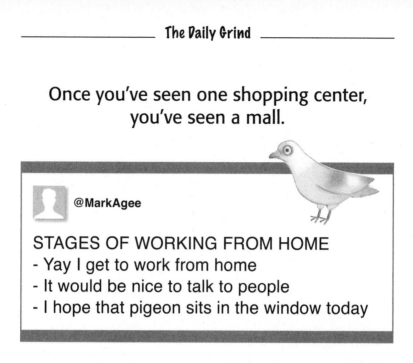

@MarkAgee

STAGES OF WORKING FROM HOME
- Yay I get to work from home
- It would be nice to talk to people
- I hope that pigeon sits in the window today

The state treasurer had to balance the budget, so he sliced a little bit off the proposed spending figures for schools, parks, and other services. It was the most successful fund razor of the year.

Monica is obsessed with monorails. All she ever talks about is monorails—especially how amazing it is that they zip along on just that single rail. She's got a one-track mind.

Q: When do a dentist's patients feel dumb?
A: After having their wisdom teeth removed.

A dentist and a manicurist had a rough marriage. They fought tooth and nail.

Politicians and diapers should both be changed regularly... and for the same reason.

Q: When do bakers share their secret bread recipes?
A: On a knead-to-know basis.

Q: Why did Archimedes leap from the bathtub and shout, "Eureka!"?
A: The water was too hot.

Knock-knock!
Who's there?
Satin.
Satin who?
Satin in this meeting is boring.

Weird thing at the office—everyone is naming their food. Today I ate a sandwich named Bill.

Knock-knock!
Who's there?
Butcher.
Butcher who?
Butcher money where your mouth is.

———

Did you hear about the mime fight?
It was unspeakable!

———

A guy goes into a hardware store and asks the manager for a tool to break up some hard ground. The manager shows him a wall of shovels, hoes, and other tools and says, "Take your pick."

There was a housepainter who was always looking for a way to save a buck, so he would often thin his paint to make it go further. One day, a local church decided to do a big restoration, and this painter put in a bid. He got the job because his price was so competitive.

Just as he was finishing the job, the painter was up on a scaffold when suddenly there was a horrendous clap of thunder. The sky opened and rain poured down, washing the watery paint off the church and knocking the painter down onto the lawn, surrounded by puddles of the thinned and useless paint.

Fearing this was a judgment from the Almighty, he got on his knees and cried, "Forgive me! What should I do?"

And from the thunder, a mighty voice spoke: "Repaint! Repaint and thin no more!"

The quarter refused to jump off the train with the nickel. It had more cents.

"Why is the man who invests all your money called a 'broker'?"

—George Carlin

Q: Why didn't the approaching black hole concern the astronaut?

A: He just didn't understand the gravity of the situation.

A rope walks into a bar. The bartender squints at him and says, "A rope? We don't serve your kind here. Get out!"

The rope goes outside, ties himself into a bow, messes up his edges, and walks back into the bar.

"Aren't you that rope that just came in here?" the bartender asks.

"Nope," says the rope, "I'm a frayed knot."

A mushroom walks into a bar. The bartender says, "We don't serve mushrooms here."

The mushroom responds, "Why not? I'm a fungi!"

A panda walks into a restaurant, sits down, and orders a sandwich. After he finishes the sandwich, he pulls out a gun, shoots the waiter, and then stands up to leave.

"Hey!" shouts the manager. "Where are you going? You just shot my waiter, and you didn't pay for your sandwich!"

"Hey man, I'm a *panda*! Look it up!"

The manager opens his dictionary and sees the following definition for panda: "A tree-dwelling marsupial of Asian origin, characterized by distinct black and white coloring. Eats shoots and leaves."

A neutron walks into a bar and orders a beer. The bartender promptly serves up a cold one. "How much?" asks the neutron.

"For you?" replies the bartender, "No charge."

Please don't
text for the
next hour.
I'm in a
meeting.

I wasn't
gonna.

What did I
just say?!

Two fleas walk out of a bar.
"Should we walk or take the dogs?"

Q: What's a missionary's favorite kind of car?
A: A convertible.

Q: What does a philosophical dolphin say?
A: "What is my porpoise?"

At the height of his career, Elvis was in a nightclub in Las Vegas having a drink when a fan approached him.

"Elvis, would you come by that table over there and say, 'Hey, how've you been?' to me?"

Elvis declined. "I'm just trying to relax here."

"Please? I'm a huge fan, and it would really impress my date."

Reluctantly, Elvis agreed. A few minutes later, he approached the table. "Hey! How've you been?" he asked.

"Elvis! Can't you see I'm busy?"

Q: Why do trees hate tests?
A: The questions always stump them.

Without geometry, life is pointless.

Q: What did one wall say to the other wall?
A: I'll meet you at the corner.

Parallel lines have so much in common.
It's a shame they'll never meet.

I support both math and farming.
I guess you could say I'm pro-tractor.

A bear walks into a restaurant and says,
"I'd like a grilled...............cheese."
   "What's with the big pause?" the
bartender asks.
   "I'm a bear."

A screwdriver walks into a bar, and the
bartender says, "Hey, we have a drink named
after you!"
   "Really?" the screwdriver replies, surprised.
"You have a drink named Steve?"

Knock-knock!
Who's there?
Amarillo.
Amarillo who?
Amarillo-fashioned
cowboy!

I interviewed for a job as a blacksmith. The guy asked me if I had ever shoed a horse. I said, "No, but I've told a donkey to go away."

Jake goes into a pet shop to buy a parrot. The shop owner points to three identical parrots on a perch and says, "The parrot on the left costs $500."

"Why does it cost so much?" Jake asks.

"Well," the shopkeeper replies, "that parrot knows how to use a computer."

Jake then asks about the next parrot and is told that it costs $1,000, because it can do everything the other parrot can do, plus it knows how to install a network.

Naturally, Jake asks about the third parrot. "That one is $2,000."

"Wow! What's so special about that one?"

"To be honest, I have never seen it do anything, but the other two call him boss!"

Q: Why did the bacteria cross the microscope?
A: To get to the other slide.

A thief sneaks up behind a man and sticks a pistol in his ribs. "Give me your money!"

The man, shocked by the attack, says, "You can't do that, I'm a United States congressman!"

The thief thinks for a moment and replies, "In that case, give me *my* money!"

@michelleisawolf

I bet a lot of teachers look at Facebook posts and think "oh now you wanna write an essay."

A man is trying on shoes.

"So how do they feel?" the salesclerk asks.

"They're a little too tight," the man replies.

"Well, try pulling the tongue out," the clerk suggests.

"Okay," he says. "They thtill theel a bith thoo thight."

I strung all my watches together to make a belt. It was a waist of time.

Did you hear about the world's worst thesaurus? Not only is it terrible, but it's also terrible.

Q: Where do saplings go to learn?
A: Elementree school.

Q: What did the pancake learn in music class?
A: B-flat.

Have you heard the one about the researcher who was reading a book on helium? She just couldn't put it down.

Q: What is a witch's favorite subject in school?
A: Spelling.

Einstein developed a theory about space.
And it was about time, too!

Thanks for explaining the word "copious"
to me. It means a lot.

Q: Why don't calculus majors party?
A: Because you can't drink and derive.

Q: What did one math book say to the other?
A: "Look, buddy, I've got my own problems."

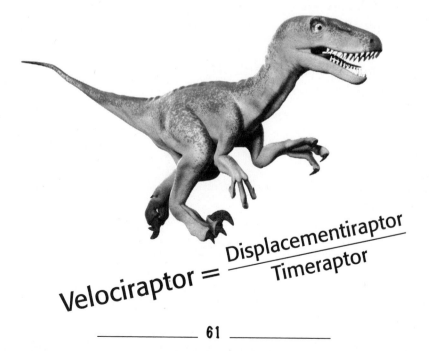

$$\text{Velociraptor} = \frac{\text{Displacementiraptor}}{\text{Timeraptor}}$$

Q: How can you tell when you're in a math teacher's garden?
A: All the trees have square roots.

Do you know who invented fractions?
Henry the 1/8.

There's a fine line between a
numerator and a denominator.
(Only a fraction of people get this joke.)

Late one night, a man is driving down the road, speeding. A police officer pulls him over. The cop says to the man, "Are you aware of how fast you were going?"

The man replies, "Yes, I am. I'm trying to escape a robbery I got involved in."

The cop gives him a skeptical look and says, "You were robbed?"

The man casually replies, "No, I committed the robbery."

The cop is shocked. "So, you're telling me you were speeding, and you committed a robbery?"

"Yes," the man says calmly. "I have the loot in the back."

The officer responds, "Sir, place your hands on the dashboard. I need your license and registration." He reaches in the window.

"Don't do that!" the man yells fearfully. "You'll find the gun in my glove compartment!" The cop withdraws his hand. "Wait here," he says.

The cop calls for backup. Soon, police cars and helicopters flood the area. The man is cuffed quickly and taken to a police car. However, before he gets in, a cop walks up to him and says, while gesturing to the cop that pulled him over, "Sir, this officer informed us that you had committed a robbery, had stolen loot in the trunk of your car, and had a loaded gun in your glove compartment. However, we found none of these things in your car."

The man replies, "Yeah, and I bet that liar said I was speeding, too!"

I'd tell you a chemistry joke,
but I don't know if I'll get a reaction.

Q: What do you do with a dead chemist?
A: You barium.

No matter how hard you push the envelope, it'll still be stationery.

Q: What was Forrest Gump's password?
A: 1forrest1

Did you hear about the restaurant on the moon?
  The food is great but there's no atmosphere.

Q: How does NASA organize a party?
A: They planet.

Jessa said she knew me from the vegetarian restaurant, but I'd never met herbivore.

A man is on a long journey with his horse and his dog. The dog stops and says, "I can't go on! I need water."

The astonished man says, "Whoa! I didn't know you could talk!"

The horse turns its head: "Me neither!"

Q: Why do ghosts hang out at bars?
A: Because they like boos.

Knock-knock!
Who's there?
Marmoset.
Marmoset who?
Marmoset there'd be days like this.

Want to hear a joke about paper?
Never mind, it's tearable.

Q: What do you call a kid fortune-teller who ran away from school?
A: A small medium at large.

@peachesanscream

The sexiest fantasy in 50 Shades Of Grey is the bit where she gets a job in journalism without having to do years of unpaid work experience.

A thief fell and broke his leg in wet cement. It turned him into a hardened criminal.

Did you hear the one about the unstamped letter? You wouldn't get it.

I was having dinner with Bobby Fischer over a checkered tablecloth. It took him two hours to pass the salt.

Tom was excited about his promotion to vice president of his company. He bragged about it to his wife for weeks on end. Finally, she couldn't take it any longer, and told him, "Listen, it means nothing, they even have a vice president of peas at the grocery store!"

"Really?" he said. Unsure if this was true, Tom decided to call the grocery store.

A clerk answered, and Tom said, "Can I please talk to the vice president of peas?"

"Canned or frozen?"

Some sad news out of Australia today.
The inventor of the boomerang grenade died.

A koala should be classified as a bear.
It has all the koalaifications!

Q: What do you call an alligator in a vest?
A: An investigator.
Q: What do you call a crocodile in a vest?
A: A silly-looking crocodile.

First Mate: Feeding the prisoners to the sharks isn't any fun.
Captain: It is for the sharks!

"My mother told me I would never amount to anything because I procrastinate. I said, 'Just wait.'"

—Judy Tenuta

Q: Why did the traffic light turn red?
A: You would too, if you had to change in the middle of the street.

Today someone knocked on the door and asked for a small donation for the local public swimming pool. I gave him a glass of water.

Q: Why did Humpty Dumpty have a great fall?
A: He was compensating for his lousy summer.

Q: Why shouldn't you loan money to anthropologists?
A: They consider a million years ago to be recent.

@KeetPotato

my boss: [whispering into my coffin] "you haven't submitted your timesheet"

Grandpa: Sonny boy, today is the first day of your life!
Grandson: Then what was yesterday?

I was up all night looking for the sun.
Then it dawned on me.

HUMOR IN THE HOUSE
Family Life and Creature Comforts

Q: When does a joke become a dad joke?
A: When the punch line becomes apparent.

My daughter is smarter than Abraham Lincoln. She can recite the Gettysburg Address, and she's only nine years old. Lincoln didn't say it until he was 50!

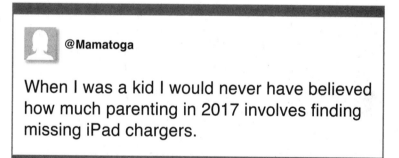

@Mamatoga

When I was a kid I would never have believed how much parenting in 2017 involves finding missing iPad chargers.

Teacher: Did your father help you with your homework?
Kid: No, he did it all by himself!

Mom: I thought you said you were running away with the circus.
Daughter: I did, but the police made me bring it back.

In a hurry while taking his son to school, a man made a U-turn at a red light.

"Uh-oh, I just made an illegal turn!" the man said.

"Aw, Dad, it's probably okay," the son said. "The police car behind us just did the same thing."

Teenager's dad: Have her back by 8:15.
Daughter's boyfriend: The middle of August? Great!

I spent a lot of time, money, and effort childproofing my house, but the kids still get in.

A lifeguard told a mother to make her young son stop peeing in the pool. "Oh, what's the big deal?" the mother protested. "All kids from time to time will pee in a pool."

"Oh really?" asked the lifeguard. "From the diving board?"

Did you hear about the marble statue that left her husband? She was tired of being taken for granite.

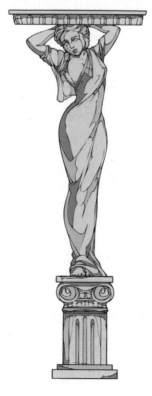

Child: Nanna, I'm a chubby old man.
Grandmother: What did you say?
Child: I'm a chubby old man.
Grandmother: Now, why would you say something like that?
Child: Well, everybody says I look just like my daddy.

"My wife said to me, 'If you won the lottery, would you still love me?' I said, 'Of course I would. I'd miss you, but I'd still love you.'"

—Frank Carson

My dog used to chase people on a scooter a lot. It got so bad we had to take his scooter away.

Dad: Why is your January report card so bad?
Kid: Things are always marked down after Christmas.

Q: What do you call a small mother?
A: A minimum.

For weeks a kindergartner excitedly told his teacher that he was going to have a baby sister. One day his mother let him feel her belly while the unborn baby was kicking. The kid was speechless. He didn't say anything about his sister for days after, leading his teacher to ask how she was coming along. The kid burst into tears and cried out, "Mommy ate it!"

Did you hear about the twins who got an apartment together? Before they were roommates they were wombmates.

A man was traveling down a country road when he saw a large group of people outside a house. He stopped and asked someone why the crowd was there.

"Joe's mule kicked his mother-in-law and she died," said a farmer.

"Wow, she must have been pretty popular," he replied.

"No," the farmer said, "we're all here to bid on that mule."

The Best Dad

Hey dad can you bring some lunch for me today?

Hello?

Are you ignoring me?

I'm pregnant.

What?!?!

Just kidding. I just wanted to get your attention. Bring me food!

Father: I want to take my son out of this terrible math class.
Teacher: But he's top of the class.
Father: That's why it must be a terrible class.

Knock-knock!
Who's there?
Dew.
Dew who?
Dew something about your room,
it's a mess.

Q: What did the baby corn say to the mama corn?
A: "Where's Popcorn?"

A teenager was having trouble learning to balance his new checking account.

His mom informed him, "The bank returned the check you wrote to the sporting goods store."

"Oh, good," he said. "I can use it to buy a new iPad!"

Q: What does a panda fry its bamboo in?
A: A pan, duh.

A husband tells his wife, "Since it's your birthday, remember that red Lamborghini that you really wanted?" The wife screams in joy, and then the husband says, "Well, I got you a toothbrush, same color. Happy birthday!"

Dad: Sorry, but I only know how to make two dishes: meat loaf and apple pie.
Kid: Which one is this?

Our family is like a fine cheese.
We get funkier with age.

Q: What did the hippie tell his friend who said he couldn't stay on his couch anymore?
A: "Namaste."

@iwearaonesie

watching the kids play hide and seek in the park and mine just hid behind a chain link fence

at least we don't have to save for college

My wife always skips a letter when she sings the alphabet. And she never says Y.

Pride is what you feel when your kids net $100 from a garage sale.
Panic is what you feel when you realize your car is missing.

A woman was shopping in the mall with her four-year-old kid. A display in the window of a lingerie store caught her eye.

"Do you think Daddy would like this?" she asked, pointing to the lacy pajamas with matching robe.

"No way," the child replied. "Daddy would *never* wear that."

Wife: I thought we agreed on three beers and be home by ten.

Husband: I'm sorry, honey, I always get those two mixed up.

Kid: So, how are you liking your cell phone?

Kid: Mom?

Kid: Why aren't you answering?

Mom: Howdoyoudoaspace

Did you hear about the houses next door to each other that fell in love?
 It's a lawn-distance relationship.

I don't trust those trees in our yard.
 They're shady.

When I want to call a family meeting, I just turn off the WiFi and wait for them all to gather.

A man speaks frantically into the phone. "My wife is pregnant, and her contractions are only two minutes apart!"

"Is this her first child?" the doctor queries.

"No, you idiot!" the man shouts. "This is her husband!"

Q: How does a penguin build a house?
A: Igloos it together.

The clouds parted and a voice thundered, "Come forth, and you will receive eternal life."

But John came fifth, so he just got a toaster.

That's a nice ham you've got there, son! It'd be a shame if someone put an "s" at the front, and an "e" at the end.

Kid: I need to go, I have a bus to catch.
Dad: How are you going to do that? They're massive.

Knock-knock!
Who's there?
Avenue.
Avenue who?
Avenue learned
to wash
your hands
before dinner?

Knock-knock!
Who's there?
Candy.
Candy who?
Candy kid ever learn to clean up his room?

Husband: Whisper dirty things to me.
Wife: The garage, the driveway, your car…

A little girl fell into a well, and although she cried for help, her brother stood by and did nothing. Finally, the next-door neighbor came over and pulled the girl out.

"Why didn't you help her?" the neighbor asked the boy.

He replied, "How could I be her brother and assist her, too?"

Q: What did the father buffalo say to his son when he left for school?
A: "Bison."

@wolfpuppy

a dog slowly rolls past you in a red plastic baby car. this is a bad neighborhood

Q: What do you get if you cross a sheepdog with a rose?
A: A collie-flower.

I believe that we parents must encourage our children to become educated, so they can get into a good college that we cannot afford.

—Dave Barry

Four expectant fathers are waiting in a Minneapolis hospital maternity ward while their wives are in labor.

The nurse comes in and tells the first man, "Congratulations! You're the father of twins!"

"What a coincidence!" he says. "I work for the Minnesota Twins baseball team!"

The nurse returns and tells the second man, "Your wife just had triplets!"

"Wow, what a coincidence! I work for 3M Company!"

Then the nurse tells the third man that he and his wife now have quadruplets.

"Another coincidence! I work at the Four Seasons Hotel!"

At this point, the fourth guy faints. When he comes to, the others ask what's wrong. "What's wrong?! I work for 7 Up!"

I asked my wife to pick up a pumpkin to make pumpkin pie. When she said she couldn't find one at the store, I told her, "I guess our plans are squashed."

A father passing by his son's bedroom was astonished to see the bed was nicely made, and everything was picked up. Then he saw an envelope, propped up prominently on the pillow. It was addressed to "Dad." With a gut-wrenching feeling, he opened the envelope and read the letter with trembling hands.

Dear Dad,

It is with great regret and sorrow that I'm writing you. I had to elope with my new girlfriend, because I wanted to avoid a scene with you and Mom.

I've been finding real passion with Stacy, and she is so nice, but I knew you would not approve of her because of her piercings, tattoos, tight motorcycle clothes, and because she is so much older than I am.

But it's not only the passion, Dad. She's pregnant. Stacy said that we will be very happy. She owns a trailer in the woods and has a stack of firewood for the whole winter. We share a dream of having many more children.

Don't worry, Dad. I'm 15, and I know how to take care of myself. Someday, I'm sure we'll be back to visit, so you can get to know your many grandchildren.

Love, your son,
Joshua

P.S. Dad, none of the above is true. I'm over at Jason's house. I just wanted to remind you that there are worse things in life than the report card that's on the kitchen table. Call when it's safe for me to come home!

Q: What do you call a woman who always knows where her husband is?
A: A widow.

> **@josswhedon**
>
> I'm disgusted when I see some old guy with a younger woman. Or a younger guy with a younger woman. Just couples. Or groups. Any person.

Kid: Dad, are bugs good to eat?
Dad: Let's not talk about those things at the dinner table.

20 minutes later…

Dad: Now, what did you want to know?
Kid: Oh, never mind. There was a bug in your soup, but now it's gone.

Teacher (on phone): You say Michael has a cold and can't come to school today? To whom am I speaking?
Voice: This is my father.

Q: What's the difference between a high-hit baseball and a maggot's father?
A: One's a pop fly. The other's a fly pop.

Being a great father is like shaving.
No matter how good you shaved today,
you have to do it again tomorrow.

"You missed a spot."

I'm a parent, so I'm always right.
There was one time I thought I was wrong.
But as it turns out, I was wrong.

Q: How is a dog like
a phone?
A: It has collar ID.

A father was trying to teach his young son
the evils of alcohol. He put one worm in a
glass of water and another worm in a glass of
whiskey. The worm in the water lived, while
the one in the whiskey curled up and died.

"All right, Son," asked the father, "what does
that show you?"

"It shows that if you drink alcohol, you will
not have worms."

Knock-knock!
Who's there?
Ozzie.
Ozzie who?
Ozzie you sneaking in after curfew.

A little girl notices some strands of her mother's hair are turning white. "Mom," she asks, "Why is your hair turning white?"

Annoyed, her mother responds, "Because I have a little girl who is constantly making trouble and causing me to worry."

The little girl thinks about it for a few minutes and says, "So why is Grandma's hair all white?"

Eric gets engaged, and he can't wait to show off his future wife. He says to his mother, "I'm going to bring home three girls, and I want you to guess which one is my fiancée."

Twenty minutes later, Eric walks in the door with three ladies.

"It's that one," says his mother without blinking an eye.

"Holy cow!" exclaims Eric. "How in the world did you know it was her?"

"I just don't like her."

Knock-knock!
Who's there?
Hertz.
Hertz who?
You only Hertz the one you love.

Q: What's the difference between in-laws and outlaws?
A: Outlaws are wanted.

Kid: I'm really worried. My dad works 12 hours a day to give me a nice home and food on the table. My mom spends the whole day cleaning and cooking for me. I'm worried sick!
Friend: What have you got to worry about? Sounds to me like you've got it made!
Kid: What if they try to escape?

@BoobsRadley

I bet the worst part of dating a documentary filmmaker is when he brings up things you did in the past and sets them to banjo music.

Q: What's brown, wrinkled, and lives in a tower?
A: The Lunch Bag of Notre Dame.

Kid: Dad, how much does it cost to get married?
Dad: I don't know. I'm still paying for it.

A couple went to the doctor for the first time after finding out the wife was pregnant. The doctor took out a tiny stamp and stamped the woman's stomach with it. The couple was curious about what the stamp was for, so when they got home, the husband got out his magnifying glass. In very tiny letters, the stamp said, "When you can read this, come back and see me."

I never let my kid watch an orchestra on TV. There's just too much sax and violins.

Daughter: Where are the Himalayas?
Father: If you'd clean your room, you'd know where to find things!

A guy is sitting at home when he hears a knock at the door. He opens the door and is surprised to see a snail on the porch. He picks up the snail and throws it as far as he can.

Three years later, there's a knock on the door. He opens it, and sees the same snail.

The snail says angrily, "Well, what was *that* all about?"

Child: Dad, why do you write so slow?
Dad: I'm a slow reader.

A man and his daughter were at the zoo. They were watching the tigers, and the father was talking about how ferocious they are.

"Daddy, if the tigers got out and ate you up—"

"Oh, honey, don't worry about that."

"—which bus would I take home?"

A Scottish mother visits her son in his New York City apartment and asks, "How do you like the Americans, Donald?"

"Mother," says Donald, "they're such noisy people. One neighbor won't stop banging his head against the wall, while the other screams and screams all night long."

"Oh, Donald! How do you manage to put up with them?"

"What can I do? I just lie in bed quietly, playing my bagpipes."

Q: What's a bad night for a tree?
A: Three Dog Night.

I once gave my husband the silent treatment for an entire week, at the end of which he declared, "Hey, we've been getting along great lately!"

A child psychologist had twin boys—one was an optimist and the other a pessimist. Just to see what would happen, on Christmas Eve he loaded the pessimist's room with toys and games. In the optimist's room, he dumped a pile of horse droppings.

The next morning, the father found the pessimist surrounded by his gifts, crying. "What's wrong?" the father asked.

"I have a ton of game manuals to read. I need batteries. And eventually, all my toys will be broken!" sobbed the pessimist.

Passing the optimist's room, the father saw the boy cheering and dancing for joy around the pile of manure. "Why are you so happy?" he asked.

"Well," the boy gushed, "there's got to be a pony in here somewhere!"

_____

Q: How is a baby bird like its dad?
A: It's a chirp off the old block.

Yesterday I asked my wife what she wanted for her upcoming birthday. She told me she wants something with a lot of diamonds. I sure hope she likes the deck of cards I bought her.

———

❝I just bought a new house. It has no plumbing. It's un-can-ny.❞

—Morey Amsterdam

———

Q: Did you hear about the haunted French pancakes?
A: They'll give you the crepes!

———

Q: What happened when the dog ate the firefly?
A: It barked with de-light!

John was at his family reunion when Raylee, his second cousin, said, "You look terrible. What's the matter?"

"My mother died in June," he said, "and she left me $10,000."

"Gee, that's tough," Raylee replied. "I'm sorry for your loss."

"Then in July," John continued, "my father died, leaving me $50,000."

"Wow. Both of your parents gone in two months. It's been a rough year for you. It will get better."

"And last month my aunt Sylvie died, and left me $15,000."

"Three family members lost in three months? Wow. I don't even know what to say."

"Then this month," John continued, "nothing!"

..... Dog

The Postman's coming up the path.

He thinks he's going to deliver some letters.

He forgot one thing.

BATDOG.

You better not be on the garage roof again.

Therapist: So why do you want to end your marriage?
Her: I'm sick of all his *Star Wars* jokes.
Him: Divorce is strong with this one.

 @Peachesanscream

New boyfriend is allergic to kitten so can't keep him :(He's ginger & named Tom. Friendly. Comes when called. 28yrs-old & works in IT.

My wife told me I didn't know what irony is. It was ironic, because we were at a bus stop.

Knock-knock!
Who's there?
Albee.
Albee who?
Well Albee a monkey's uncle.

Q: What color do cats like best?
A: Purrrrple.

This morning my wife yelled at me, "You aren't even listening to me, are you?" I couldn't help but think, *What a rude way to start a conversation.*

"Dad, will the pizza be long?"
"No, it will probably be round."

Q: What do you use to keep your ig from falling off?
A: Igloo.

My wife and I decided not to have kids. The kids are taking it pretty hard.

Knock-knock!
Who's there?
Donohue.
Donohue who?
Donohue think you can
hide your grades from me!

 @baddadjokes

When my wife told me to stop impersonating a flamingo I had to put my foot down.

Four years ago today, I asked out the girl of my dreams. Today, I asked her to marry me. She said no both times.

Q: What did the mama cow say to the baby cow?
A: "It's pasture bedtime."

My grandfather was an honorable,
brave man. He had the heart of a lion,
and a lifetime ban from the zoo.

Q: What did the banana do when it saw a
horde of hungry monkeys?
A: Split!

My wife said I was immature.
So I told her to get out of my fort.

Q: What do you call your dad when he falls through the ice?
A: A Pop-sicle.

The strangest part about picking out a name for your child is realizing how many people you hate.

Father: I know what's causing your bad grades. You're spending too much time watching television.
Kid: I'm sorry, you'll have to phrase that in the form of a question.

Q: Which food should you only eat in the bathroom?
A: Showerkraut.

Time flies like an arrow.
Fruit flies like a banana.

Q: Which day
do eggs hate?
A: Fry-day.

"Why is the bride wearing all white?" a little girl asked her mother at a wedding.

"White is the color of purity and happiness, and today is the bride's happiest day," her mother tells her.

The little girl thinks for a moment and then asks, "So why is the groom wearing all black?"

Did you hear about the two antennas that got married?

The wedding was terrible, but the reception was great.

Kid: Dad, can you teach me how to play chess?
Dad: Sure, let me pick up a board at the pawn shop.

Q: Why was the piano on the porch?
A: Because it forgot its keys.

I told my wife she was drawing her eyebrows on too high. She looked surprised.

From a comedy routine by
George Burns and Gracie Allen:

George: Gracie, what day is it today?
Gracie: Well, I don't know.
George: You can find out if you look at that paper on your desk.
Gracie: Oh, George, that doesn't help. It's yesterday's paper.

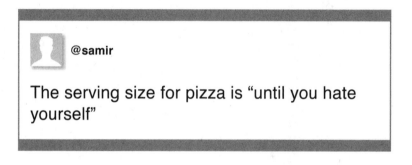

@samir

The serving size for pizza is "until you hate yourself"

A cannibal invites a friend over for dinner. As they're nibbling on the appetizer, the guest says, "Wow, your wife makes a lovely stew."

"I know," answers the host. "I sure will miss her."

Q: What do you call a shoe made out of a banana?
A: A slipper!

Knock-knock!
Who's there?
Yoda.
Yoda who?
Yoda one who's supposed to do the dishes.

Q: What did Adam say on the day before Christmas?
A: "It's Christmas, Eve."

Wife: What are you doing? You've been reading our marriage certificate for an hour.
Husband: I was looking for the expiration date.

Q: Where do single cats advertise for a date?
A: The purr-sonal ads.

Q: How do cats mail letters?
A: Using fur-class mail.

@KeetPotato

[ordering cake over phone]
"and what would you like the cake to say?"
[covers phones to ask wife]
"do we want a talking cake?"

One day a man went to an auction to buy a parrot. He really wanted it, but he kept getting outbid. So, he bid higher…and higher…and higher. Even though he had to bid way more than he intended, he finally won the bird. As he was paying for it, he said to the auctioneer, "I sure hope this parrot can talk. I'd hate to have paid this much to find out that he can't!"

"Don't worry," replied the auctioneer. "Who do you think kept bidding against you?"

Q: Who writes nursery rhymes and squeezes oranges?
A: Mother Juice.

I put my "I Voted" sticker in my beard
and told my wife that someone
was going to win by a whisker.

Knock-knock!
Who's there?
Kumquat.
Kumquat who?
Kumquat may, I'll always love you.

Q: Who is a dog's favorite comedian?
A: Growlcho Marx.

A dog walks into a telegraph office and finds a bored clerk sitting behind the desk. The clerk looks at the dog and asks, "Are you here to send a telegram?" The dog paws at the ground and barks.

The clerk laughs and says, "Okay, what message do you want to send?"

The dog barks: "Woof woof woof woof woof woof woof woof!"

The clerk writes it down and then offers, "You know, for the same price, you can fit one more 'woof' in there."

The dog gives him a puzzled look and says, "But then it wouldn't make any sense."

Did you hear about the dad who is so lazy that he just puts coffee grounds in his mustache and drinks hot water?

A baby horse started cussing at its mother.
He was using some very foal language.

@ch000ch

hi, grandma? can u come pick me up from my rap battle? It's over. no, i lost. he saw u drop me off & did a pretty devastating rhyme about it.

Q: What kind of dog does Dracula have?
A: A bloodhound.

Q: Why do seagulls live by the sea?
A: If they lived by the bay they'd be bagels.

Knock-knock!
Who's there?
Kelp.
Kelp who?
Kelp me get a gift for your mom.

Did you hear about the new broom model they just put out?

It's sweeping the nation.

Q: Why did the rope get put in time-out?
A: Because he was very knotty.

This doormat is looking old.
I think it's worn out its welcome.

Have you heard the joke about the roof?
Never mind, it's over your head.

@RockabillyJay

Young children are like sponges. They are the filthiest thing in your house.

Gracie Allen: The baby my father brought home was a little French baby. So, my mother took up French.
George Burns: Why?
Gracie Allen: So she would be able to understand the baby.

Knock-knock!
Who's there?
Gucci.
Gucci who?
Gucci-gucci-goo!

Knock-knock!
Who's there?
Waddle.
Waddle who?
Waddle we do about this kid?

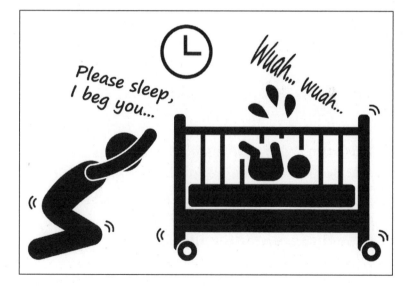

An old man in Reno calls his son in New York the day before Thanksgiving. He says, "I hate to ruin your day, Son, but I have to tell you that your mother and I are divorcing. Forty-five years of marriage is enough."

"Pop, what are you talking about?!" the son exclaims.

"We can't stand the sight of each other any longer," his father says, "and I'm sick of talking about this, so *you* call your sister in Chicago and tell her."

Frantic, the son calls his sister, who explodes on the phone. "Like heck, they're getting divorced!" she shouts. "I'll take care of this."

She calls and immediately reprimands her father. "You are *not* getting divorced!" she says. "Don't do a single thing until I get there. I'm calling my brother back, and we'll both be there tomorrow. Until then, don't do a thing, do you hear me?" And she hangs up.

The old man turns to his wife. "Okay," he says, "they're coming for Thanksgiving and paying their own way."

@baddadjokes

My wife is on a tropical food diet, the house is full of the stuff. It's enough to make a mango crazy.

Q: What's a dog's favorite city?
A: New Yorkie.

Q: What breed of dog loves to take baths?
A: A shampoodle.

If towels could tell jokes, I bet they would have a dry sense of humor.

Q: Which food stays hot in the fridge?
A: Hot dogs.

 @Smoohead

When making meals for toddlers, I find it best to throw whatever you make directly in the trash and give them a piece of cheese

Q: What do you call a cow who's just given birth?
A: De-calf-inated!

A cow that doesn't produce milk is an udder failure.

An old man wanted to plant a tomato garden, but it was difficult work, and his only son, Vincent, was in prison. The old man described the predicament in a letter:

"Dear Vincent,
Looks like there will be no tomatoes this year. I'm just too old to be digging. I wish you were here to dig it for me.
Love, Dad"

A week later, he received a response:

"Dear Dad,
Sorry I'm not there to help, but whatever you do, don't dig up that garden. That's where I buried the bodies.
Love, Vincent"

Soon, FBI agents arrived and dug up the entire area. But they couldn't find any bodies. They apologized and left. The next day, the old man received another letter:

"Dear Dad,
Go ahead and plant the tomatoes now. That's the best I could do under the circumstances.
Love, Vinnie"

True story: A man had an old telephone booth in his living room. The phone didn't work, but it was quite a conversation piece.

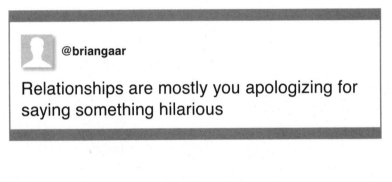

@briangaar

Relationships are mostly you apologizing for saying something hilarious

Did you hear the joke about
the pepperoni pizza?
Never mind. It's way too cheesy.

I was so ugly my mother used to feed me with a slingshot.

—Rodney Dangerfield

Q: What do you call a horse and bee that live in the same neighborhood?
A: Neigh-buzz.

The Leaning Tower of Pisa and the tower of Big Ben were thinking of starting a family, but they called it off.

One didn't have the time, and the other didn't have the inclination.

Mom

please stop changing the google logo so much

I like the original one

Mom I don't change the logo. Google changes it.

on my computer

You don't run the google?

If I did I wouldn't be driving a 2004 ford.

Q: Where should you never take a dog?
A: The flea market.

Show me a piano falling down a mineshaft,
and I'll show you A flat minor.

 @okimstillhungry

Her: *looking deeply in my eyes* Lets say
what we're thinking about at the same time
Me: Ok ready, go
Her: I love y-
Me: Crunchwrap supreme

Q: When's a door not a door?
A: When it's ajar.

I wrote a song about a tortilla.
Well, actually, it's more of a wrap.

On Father's Day, a little boy decides to make his dad breakfast in bed. He makes scrambled eggs, toast, and coffee. He brings it to his dad, hands him a cup of coffee, and says, "Try it, Dad!" The father takes a sip and nearly gags because it is so strong. The little boy asks, "Dad, how do you like it?"

Trying not to hurt his feelings, the dad replies, "This is…something else, I've never tasted coffee quite like this before, Son."

The little boy smiles from ear to ear and says, "Drink some more!"

As the father is drinking, he notices two army men in the bottom of the cup. "Hey! Why did you put army men in here?"

The little boy again smiles and sings, "The Best Part of Waking Up Is *Soldiers* in Your Cup!"

Q: What starts with a T, ends with a T, and is full of T?

A: A teapot.

Being a parent means knowing how to unwrap a candy bar without making any noise.

A man stumbled out his front door and immediately passed out on his porch. A neighbor saw and called 911. When the paramedics arrived, they helped him regain consciousness and asked if he knew what caused him to faint. "It was enough to make anybody faint," he said. "My teenaged son asked me for the keys to the garage, and instead of driving the car out, he came out with the lawn mower and started mowing the yard."

 @yoyoha

Parenting is mostly just informing kids how many more minutes they have of something.

Kid: Dad, make me a sandwich.
Dad: Poof, you're a sandwich!

Q: What's the difference between a mom and a dad?

A: If you've got a nasty allergic reaction, Mom will want to take you to the hospital. Dad will wait and see because he doesn't want to make any rash decisions.

Kid: Why did the chicken cross the road?
Dad: I don't know, ask your mother.

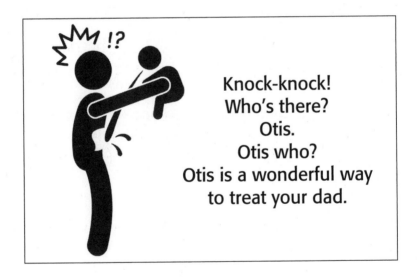

Knock-knock!
Who's there?
Otis.
Otis who?
Otis is a wonderful way
to treat your dad.

66When my kids become wild and unruly, I use a nice safe playpen. When they're finished, I climb out.99

—Erma Bombeck

Q: What did Santa say when he fell down a chimney backward?
A: "Oh! Oh! Oh!"

A six-year-old boy called his mother from his friend Chad's house and confessed he had broken a lamp when he threw a football in their living room.

"But, Mom," he said, brightening, "you don't have to worry about buying another one. Chad's mother said it was irreplaceable."

Q: What does an alligator get on welfare?
A: Gatorade.

Burnt my Hawaiian pizza last night.
I should've put it on aloha setting.

Rule of thumb: Children who go to bed early, get up early. Children who go to bed late, get up early.

@Kim_pulsive

Lorde wrote her Grammy nominated album at age 14. My son is 13 and has let the bathtub overflow twice while he was sitting INSIDE of it.

Q: What's the fastest way for a parent to get their kid's attention?
A: Sit down and look comfortable.

Kid: I want a quesadilla.
Dad: Wow, a whole case? Why don't you start with one and go from there?

.....

Momisannoying

Don't forget to unload the dishwasher

Did you finish your homework?

We have to go to your grandmother's house for Thanksgiving.

Dad and I talked, we are going to buy you a car next month.

U are??? Omg thank u

No. We're not. I just wanted to make sure you were still getting my texts.

That was cruel.

Q: How does Davey Crockett like his pie?
A: Alamo-d.

Q: Why did the bigamist cross the road?
A: To get to the other bride.

It was an emotional wedding.
Even the cake was in tiers.

Q: Did you hear about the crazy pancake?
A: He just flipped!

Knock-knock!
Who's there?
Fanny.
Fanny who?
Fanny-body knocks, I'm not home.

@yenniwhite

1st child goals: all food is homemade, do several Mommy and Me classes, hover so she doesn't get hurt
2nd: get most of lint off fruit snack

Q: Why do you go to bed at night?
A: Because the bed can't come to you!

I used to wonder why I had hair on my legs, but now I know it's for my toddler sons and daughters to pull themselves up off the ground with as I scream in pain.

—Jim Gaffigan

My grandpa would always tell me that when he was growing up, his mother would give him $1 and send him to the store. He'd come back with two loaves of bread, half a gallon of milk, a carton of eggs, and a pound of pork. He says you can't do that nowadays—there are way too many security cameras.

Q: What did the cat say to the other cat when he jumped out and scared him?
A: "Stop that! You're freaking MEOW!"

@DannyZuker

I'm constantly amazed at how different my twin daughters are. Lisa is so much more positive & confident than her sister Hog Face.

Daughter: Dad, why is there a "4" candle on the cake? I'm turning 15.
Dad: It's the only candle I had, so it's 4 your birthday.

Did you hear about the little boy who was named after his father? They called him Dad.

A father of five won a toy at a raffle. He called his kids together to ask which one should have the present.

"Who is the most obedient?" he asked. "Who never talks back to Mother? Who does everything she says?"

Five small voices answered in unison, "Okay, Dad, you get the toy."

"When you're young, you think your dad is Superman. Then you grow up, and you realize he's just a regular guy who wears a cape.

—Dave Attell

SPORTS AND LEISURE
AKA What Dads Don't Have Time For

Q: How many golfers does it take to screw in a light bulb?
A: Fore!
Q: No, really. How many golfers does it take to screw in a light bulb?
A: Five. Okay, six. Fine—it's seven!

Clint Eastwood opened a preschool.
   It's called "Go Ahead and Make My Day Care Center."

"When I grow up, I want to be a musician."
"Well, honey, you know you can't do both."

I got excited when my son joined the cross-country team. But then I learned they don't cross the country and they're back home in just a few hours.

Q: How do snowboarders introduce
  themselves?
A: "Sorry, dude!"

I'm taking part in a stair climbing competition.
  Guess I better step up my game.

It's Game 7 of the NBA Finals, and a man
makes his way to his seat at center court.
He sits down and notices that the seat next
to him is empty. He leans over and asks his
neighbor if someone is sitting there.
  The man responds, "No, the seat's empty."
  The first man exclaims, "What?! Who in their
right mind would have a seat like this for the
NBA Finals and not use it?"
  The neighbor responds, "Well, the seat is
mine, but my wife passed away and this is
the first NBA Finals we haven't been together."
  "I'm sorry to hear that. Wasn't there anyone
else, a friend or relative, that could've taken
that seat?"
  "No, they're all at the funeral."

Jay: You're looking glum.
Tom: Yeah, my doctor says I can't play football anymore.
Jay: Really? I didn't know he'd ever seen you play!

Q: Why couldn't the bicycle stand up on its own?
A: Because it's just two-tired.

Q: What are the four worst words you can hear on a golf course?
A: "It's still your turn."

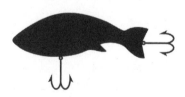

After a fish was arrested for swimming without a license, he eventually posted bail. Relieved, he said, "I'm off the hook!"

Hank didn't believe that Fred's dog could talk. So Fred asked his dog, "What's on top of a house?"

"Roof," the dog barked.

Hank wasn't convinced. So Fred asked the dog how sandpaper feels.

"Rough."

He still wasn't convinced.

"Okay, who was the greatest baseball player of all time?" Fred asked the dog.

"Ruth."

With that, Hank walked away, shaking his head. The dog turned to Fred and asked, "Does he think it's Derek Jeter?"

I forgot where I threw my boomerang.
Oh…it's coming back to me now!

Q: How many folk singers does it take to change a light bulb?

A: One to change it, and five to sing about how good the old one was.

Q: Why does Waldo always wear stripes?
A: He's afraid of getting spotted.

@neiltyson

Does it disturb anyone else that "The Los Angeles Angels" baseball team translates directly to "The The Angels Angels"?

Q: Why did the octopus blush?
A: She saw the ocean's bottom.

_____

Knock-knock!
Who's there?
Desdemona.
Desdemona who?
Desdemona Lisa still hang
in the Louvre?

There are two seasons in Canada:
winter, and poor snowmobiling season.

Q: Where does an electric cord go to shop?
A: An outlet mall.

A father and his young daughter are outside
Yankee Stadium, and the girl asks for a T-shirt
that says "Red Sox Suck." The dad hesitates,
but says, "You can have the shirt if you
promise never to say those words."

"That's right," says the vendor. "*Suck* isn't a
very nice word."

"No," replies the father. "I meant the words
Red Sox."

Four baseball fans—a Cubs fan, a Cardinals fan, a Red Sox fan, and a Yankees fan—are climbing a mountain and arguing about who loves his team more.

The Cubs fan insists he is the most loyal. "This is for the Cubs!" he yells, and jumps off the side of the mountain.

Not to be outdone, the Cardinals fan shouts, "This is for the Cardinals!" and throws himself off the mountain.

The Red Sox fan is next to profess his love for his team. He yells, "This is for everyone!" and pushes the Yankees fan off the mountain.

"Any time you need more, the money tree is here."

Q: What does BOAT stand for?

A: Bust out another thousand.

Q: What do you call a fish with no i?
A: Fsh.

A retiree is given a set of golf clubs by his coworkers. He goes to the local pro for lessons, explaining that he knows nothing about the game. The pro shows him the stance and swing, and then says, "Just hit the ball toward the flag on the first green."

The novice tees up and smacks the ball straight down the fairway and onto the green, where it stops just inches from the hole.

"Now what?" the fellow asks the speechless pro.

"Uh...you're supposed to hit it into the cup," the pro finally says.

"Oh great!" says the beginner, disgusted. "*Now* you tell me!"

Q: What did the coach say to the broken vending machine?
A: "Give me my quarterback!"

Q: What's Beethoven's favorite fruit?
A: Ba-na-na-naaaaa. Ba-na-na-*naaaaa.*

What's the difference between a baseball hitter and a skydiver?
   The baseball player goes "smack!...ARGH!" A skydiver goes "ARGH!...smack!"

Tom Cruise made a movie about cooking.
   It's called *A Few Good Menus.*

Q: What kind of sickness does a martial artist get?
A: Kung flu.

I've been running as fast as I can,
but I still can't catch my breath.

_____

Q: Why didn't the dog want to wrestle?
A: He was a boxer.

_____

It's well known throughout Europe that members of William Tell's family were early devotees of league bowling. They had sponsors and everything. According to historians, though, the records have been lost, so no one knows for whom the Tells bowled.

_____

Q: What cats make good bowlers?
A: Alley cats.

_____

*"I used to be quite the athlete—
big chest, hard stomach.
But that's all behind me now."*
—Bob Hope

A group of chess enthusiasts checked into a hotel and were standing in the lobby discussing their recent tournament victories. After about an hour, the manager came out of the office and asked them to disperse.

"But why?" they asked.

"Because," he said, "I can't stand chess nuts boasting in an open foyer."

Q: What do Michael Jordan and a turkey have in common?
A: They're both known for stuffing.

Q: Where do horses like to shop?
A: Old Neigh-vy.

Gordon was 26 over par by the 8th hole. He had landed a dozen balls in the water hazard, and dug himself into a trench fighting his way out of the rough. When his caddie coughed during a one-foot putt, Gordon exploded.

"You've got to be the worst caddie in the world!" he screamed.

"I doubt it," replied the caddie. "That would be too much of a coincidence."

Q: What's green, has four legs, and if it fell out of a tree, could kill you?

A: A pool table!

Why do we sing "Take Me Out to the Ball Game" when we're already there?

———————————

Four people are heading to Hawaii on a plane: a pilot, a lawyer, a priest, and a kid. Suddenly, the plane starts shaking and begins to go down. Searching around the cabin, they find only three parachutes.

"I have a family, and a daughter who's expecting!" says the pilot. Before anyone can stop him, he grabs a parachute and jumps off the plane.

The lawyer says, "Well, I'm the smartest man on earth, so I deserve to live!" He also grabs a parachute and jumps off.

Now there's only one parachute left. The priest notices this and tells the kid, "Son, go ahead and take the last one. I have lived my life."

The boy looks around the plane. "Wait, we can both live!"

"How?" the priest asks.

"Because the smartest man in the world just jumped out with my backpack."

Q: How did the chickens dance at the prom?
A: Chick-to-chick.

My girlfriend told me she was leaving me because of my obsession with the Monkees. I thought she was joking. But then I saw her face.

Q: What did the yogi tell his restless students?
A: "Don't just do something…sit there!"

A monk goes to a street fair to sell goods. A woman hands him a $20 bill. He takes the money, puts it in his cash box, and closes it.
   "Isn't there some change?" the woman asks.
   "Change must come from within."

The Beach Boys walk into a bar.
   "Round?"
   "Round."
   "Get a round?"
   "I'll get a round!"

Do you know the difference between a hunter and a fisherman?

A hunter lies in wait. A fisherman waits and lies.

```
Coach said I
broke my arm
in two places!
What will I do?

------------

I wouldn't go
back to those
two places,
that's for
sure!
```

Q: Why did the cabbage win the race?
A: Because it was a head!

If an athlete gets athlete's foot,
then an astronaut must get missile toe.

Q: Why was the hunter arrested while making breakfast?
A: The warden had found out he poached his eggs.

Q: What did the turkey say to the turkey hunter?
A: Quack! Quack! Quack!

An apple, a banana, and an orange were on the high dive. Only the banana wouldn't jump. Why? Because it was yellow.

Every morning the same bike hits me. It's a vicious cycle.

Q: What season is it when you're on a trampoline?
A: Spring!

A man has been stranded alone on a desert island for ten years. One day, he sees a speck on the horizon. He watches and waits as the speck gets closer and closer until out of the surf emerges a gorgeous woman wearing a wet suit and scuba gear. She calmly walks up to the man and asks, "How long has it been since you've had a cigarette?"

"Ten years!" he says.

She unzips a pocket on her left sleeve and pulls out a pack of cigarettes.

He takes one, lights it, takes a long drag, and says, "Man, that's good!"

Then she asks, "How long has it been since you've had a beer?"

"Ten years!" he replies.

She unzips a pocket on her right sleeve, pulls out a bottle of beer, and gives it to him.

He takes a long swig and says, "Wow, that's fantastic!"

Then she starts unzipping the longer zipper that runs down the front of her wet suit and says to him, "And how long has it been since you've had some *real* fun?"

The man replies, "Wow! Don't tell me that you've got a Jet Ski in there!"

Q: What type of music should you listen to when fishing?

A: Something catchy.

As the president of the Christopher Walken fan club, I can say with certainty that he owns the greatest poker face of all time. It helped him win the 2005 World Series of Poker even though he held only a joker, a 2 of clubs, a 7 of spades, a green number 4 from Uno, and a Monopoly "get out of jail free" card.

Q: What do you get when you cross an
Olympic swimmer with an elephant?
A: Swimming trunks.

We would tell you another swimming joke,
but it's too watered-down to be funny.

Q: Why did the yogurt go to the art exhibit?
A: Because it was cultured.

I took the shell off my racing snail,
thinking it would help him run faster.
If anything, it made him more sluggish.

Q: Why are tightrope walkers so healthy?
A: They eat a balanced diet.

Q: What do you call a bear with no ears?
A: B.

"He's great on the court," a sportswriter said of a college basketball player during an interview with his coach. "But's how's his schoolwork?"

"Why, he makes straight As," replied the coach.

"Wonderful!" said the sportswriter.

"Yeah," agreed the coach, "but his Bs are a little crooked."

Q: How do you search for Will Smith in the snow?
A: Look for fresh prints!

Did you hear about the fight that broke out at the seafood restaurant?
Two fish got battered.

The hardest part of learning to ride a bike is the pavement.

Q: Where do sheep go on vacation?
A: The Baaaaaahamas.

A loaded minivan pulled into the only remaining campsite. Four children leaped from the vehicle and began feverishly unloading gear and setting up the tent. Two kids rushed to gather firewood, while the other two and their mother set up the camp stove and cooking utensils.

A nearby camper marveled to the youngsters' father, "That, sir, is some display of teamwork."

"I have a system," the father replied. "No one goes to the bathroom until the camp is set up."

Q: Where do mice park their boats?
A: At the Hickory Dickory Dock.

I had been out drinking on St. Patrick's Day, so I took a bus home. That may not be a big deal to you, but I've never driven a bus before.

Q: What's the best kind of booze if you want to dance all night long?
A: Wild Twerky.

"I swallowed my flute, and I can't get it out!"
"Thank goodness you weren't playing the piano."

Q: What kind of music did the pilgrims listen to?
A: Plymouth rock.

Q: What do you call a potato at a hockey game?
A: A spec-tater.

Golfer: Caddiemaster, this boy you assigned me isn't even five years old!
Caddiemaster: Better for you, sir. He probably can't count past ten.

A fish ran into a concrete wall.
   It said, "Dam!"

_____

Q: What do you call a group of whales
   playing instruments?
A: An orca-stra.

@BitsAce

Invent a drink called "Responsibly" and your
advertising is set forever

Q: What does a didgeridoo?
A: Whatever it didgeriwants!

_____

Peter Pan is terrible boxer.
Whenever he throws a punch, it Neverlands.

Q: Why can't you play basketball with pigs?
A: They're ball hogs!

A father and son are playing golf together. The young man hits his tee shot, and it lands about 20 yards in front of a large pine tree blocking the green. He asks for advice.

"You know, Son," says his dad, "when I was your age, I'd hit that ball right over that tree."

So the young man digs in, swings as hard as he can, and smacks the ball right into the tree. It ricochets back and lands right in front of the two golfers.

"Of course, when I was your age," says the father, "that tree was only about ten feet tall."

Q: How many snowboarders does it take to screw in a light bulb?
A: Fifty. Three to die trying, one to actually pull it off, and 46 others to say, "Dude, I could do that!"

On the anniversary of his birth, devotees of a certain yogi asked what gifts they might bring. The yogi replied, "I wish for no gifts, only presence."

Q: How do trees get on the Internet?
A: Just like everyone else. They log in.

Q: If you are out in the forest all by yourself and a bear charges you, what should you do?
A: Pay him immediately!

Q: Why was Cinderella such a bad basketball player?
A: Because her coach was a pumpkin.

We use a really strong sunblock when we go to the beach with the kids. It's SPF 80: You squeeze the tube, and a sweater comes out.

—Lew Schneider

Did you hear about the football team that doesn't have a website?
   They can't string three Ws together.

Q: What did the hockey goalie say to his teammates?
A: "Let's get the puck out of here!"

Q: What kind of tea do hockey players drink?
A: Penaltea.

Soccer striker: I had an open goal but still I didn't score. I could kick myself.
Manager: I wouldn't bother. You'd probably miss.

———

Do you know the difference between England and a tea bag?
   A tea bag could stay in the Cup longer.

———

Q: What kind of candy do you eat on the playground?
A: Recess Pieces.

———

A duck, a skunk, and a deer went out for dinner at a restaurant. When it came time to pay, the skunk didn't have a scent, and the deer didn't have a buck, so they put the meal on the duck's bill.

———

Why does toilet paper like alpine skiing?
   Because it's the fastest way to get to the bottom.

Those who jump off a Paris bridge
are in Seine.

Q: What did the archer get when he hit
a bull's-eye?
A: One very angry bull.

My first job was at a running shoe company; I
tried but I just didn't fit in. Then, I got a job in
a gym, but they said I wasn't fit for the job.

Q: What do you call a girl in the middle of a tennis court?
A: Annette.

A group of bats, hanging on the ceiling of a cave, discovers a single bat standing upright on the floor of the cave. Surprised by this unusual behavior, they ask him, "What's wrong with you? What are you doing down there?"
  The little bat yells back, "Yoga!"

Give a man a fish, he'll eat for a day. Teach a man to fish, and he'll spend hundreds of dollars on equipment he'll use only twice a year.

Q: What do you call an unbelievable story about a basketball player?
A: A tall tale.

Golf pro: Now I want you to go through the motions without actually hitting the ball.
Student: But that's what I always do!

Q: How did the pirate become a boxing champion so fast?
A: Nobody was ready to take on his right hook.

@aparnapkin

So the NBA Finals, huh? So no more basketball ever again? Feels extreme but ok

---

Q: Why couldn't the Olympian listen to music?
A: Because he kept breaking all the records.

Several men are in the locker room when they're startled by the sound of a cell phone on a bench ringing. A man answers on speakerphone. Everyone else in the room can't help but listen.
Man: Hello?
Woman: Honey, it's me. Are you at the gym?
Man: Yes.

Woman: I'm at the mall now and found this beautiful dress. It's only $1,500. I really like it—can I buy it?

Man: Sure, go ahead if you like it that much.

Woman: I also stopped by the Audi dealership and saw the new models. I saw one that's just perfect.

Man: How much?

Woman: $60,000.

Man: Okay, but for that price I want it with all the extras.

Woman: Great! Oh, and one more thing. The house we wanted last year is back on the market. They're asking $950,000.

Man: Well, then go ahead and make a bid, but just offer $900,000, and negotiate from there.

Woman: Okay! I'll see you later! I love you!

Man: Bye. I love you, too.

The man hangs up. The other men in the locker room are looking at him in astonishment. He smiles and asks, "Whose phone is this?"

Knock-knock!
Who's there?
Disaster.
Disaster who?
Disaster be my lucky day!

Q: What concert only costs $0.45?
A: 50 Cent featuring Nickelback.

Q: What do you call a sold-out demolition derby?
A: A smashing success!

"My parents used to stuff me with candy. M&Ms, Jujubes, SweeTARTS. I don't think they wanted a child, I think they wanted a piñata."

—Wendy Liebman

Q: Why does someone who runs marathons make a good student?
A: Because education pays off in the long run.

Last year I entered the New York City Marathon. I was in last place. It was embarrassing. The guy in front of me, who was second to last, was making fun of me. He said, "Hey buddy, how does it feel to be last?"

So I replied, "Let me know," and I dropped out.

Q: Why was Cinderella dropped from the soccer team?
A: She kept running away from the ball.

Q: What's the difference between Kobe Bryant and time?
A: Time passes.

I just watched a documentary about how boats are held together. It was riveting.

Q: What do you call a drummer without a girlfriend?
A: Homeless.

@sucittaM

If I ever go missing I want my picture on a 40 oz. beer rather than a milk carton, because I want fun people to find me.

Q: What type of exercise is best for swimmers?
A: Pool-ups.

Did you know that spiders make excellent baseball players?
   They know how to catch flies!

Jesus and Moses are playing golf, and they're on the tenth hole. Moses hits the ball, and it heads straight for a pond. Just before the ball hits the water, the pond parts and the ball rolls up onto the green. Jesus tees up and hits one to roughly the same spot. Jesus's ball hits the water and skips across. All of a sudden, lightning flashes, and a ball drops from the sky. A fish swallows it, a bird picks up the fish, and the ball drops onto a turtle, which walks over to the hole and drops it in.

Moses turns to Jesus and says, "I hate it when your dad plays!"

_____

Q: Why did Beethoven get rid of all his chickens?
A: All they ever talked about was *Bach Bach Bach*.

_____

I tried to catch some fog today, but I mist.

_____

Q: Why do bees hum?
A: They don't know the words.

 A deer hunter was bragging about the biggest, strongest, heaviest deer he'd bagged the day before. "It's got enough meat to eat for the whole year," he boasted.

Just then the game warden came up and cited the man $500 for hunting without the proper tag.

"Five hundred dollars?" exclaimed the hunter. "All for a mangy, skinny, stubby, half-pint deer?"

Q: What does a boulder listen to?
A: Rock music.

Q: What is a mummy's favorite music genre?
A: Wrap.

Knock-knock!
Who's there?
Mozart.
Mozart who?
Mozart is found in museums.

A man standing on a riverbank yells to a woman on the other side, "Hey, how do I get to the other side of the river?"

"You're already on the other side!"

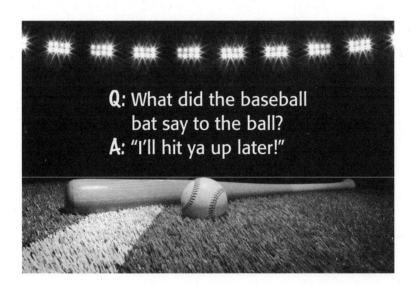

Q: What did the baseball bat say to the ball?
A: "I'll hit ya up later!"

I want my favorite team to be my pallbearers so that they can let me down one last time.

Q: Why did the coach let the elephant play basketball?
A: He had already broken the bench.

Q: Where do zombies like to vacation?
A: The Dead Sea.

Knock-knock!
Who's there?
Dion.
Dion who?
I'm dion of
thirst here!

Camping was such a chore. In spite of all of our hard work, we couldn't get the tent up. Too many missed stakes.

Q: How quiet should a bowling alley be?
A: You should be able to hear a pin drop.

Q: What is a boxer's favorite part of a joke?
A: The punch line.

Two friends are on a weekend trip. On the first day, they put on their bathing suits and head to the beach. Timothy is turning heads. The girls just can't stop staring. Justin looks at him and says, "Dude! What's your secret?"

"I keep a potato in my trunks," says Timothy. "Tomorrow, you should try it!"

So the next day they head to the beach again. This time, people see the pair and scream in disgust and run away.

"What's wrong? I put a potato in my trunks, just like you said!" says Justin.

Timothy looks at him and says, "You moron! The potato goes in front!"

The depressing thing about tennis is that no matter how good I get, I'll never be as good as a wall.

—Mitch Hedberg

Q: Why did the police go to the baseball game?
A: They heard someone stole second base.

On the way home from a hunt, a hunter stops by the grocery store. "Give me a couple of steaks," he says.

"We're out of steaks, but we have hot dogs and chicken," the butcher says.

"Hot dogs and chicken?!" yells the hunter. "How can I tell my wife I bagged a couple of hot dogs and chickens?"

Did you guys see the movie about the hot dog?
   It was an Oscar Weiner.

Two lobsters are in a tank. One turns to the other and says, "Hey, do you know how to drive this thing?

Q: What did the bowling pins do when they were mad?
A: They went on strike!

Q: What do you call an artist who makes sculptures out of bicycle parts?
A: Cycle-Angelo.

Q: Why do boxers have TGIF written on the inside of their shoes?
A: "Toes go in first."

Q: What did the flower say to the bicycle?
A: "Petal! Petal!"

A flock of geese passes overhead.

Dad: Do you know why one side of the V is longer?
Kid: No, why?
Dad: Because it has more geese.

A man is driving his SUV through the woods in the springtime. He reaches a river with a drivable bridge, but much to his surprise the river has flooded, submerging the bridge he needs to cross. He stops his car before the river, trying to figure out what to do.

He spots an old house a little bit into the woods. On the porch, a hillbilly holding a sawed-off shotgun is rocking back and forth on a chair. The driver exits his vehicle and approaches the hillbilly.

"Excuse me, sir," he asks the hillbilly. "The river nearby has flooded, and I am unable to cross. Do you know an alternate way across the river?"

The hillbilly thinks for a while, and then finally says, "Well, sir, the water ain't that deep, ya see? Probably just a couple inches high above the bridge. I'd reckon with a big rig like that, you'd make it to the other side easy."

The man thanks the hillbilly and goes back to his vehicle. He starts it up and starts driving. First, the bottom of his tires touch the water. Expecting this to be the deepest depth, he continues. Unfortunately, when his vehicle is halfway across, it is almost fully submerged. The man escapes through the window, barely making it out alive.

Furious, he returns to the hillbilly's home.

"You liar! That river was plenty deep. I lost my vehicle and I almost died!"

The hillbilly looks quite confused, and replies, "Well, that sure is strange! For the ducks, the water is only waist deep!"

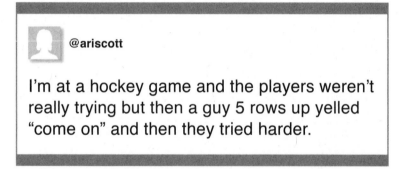

@ariscott

I'm at a hockey game and the players weren't really trying but then a guy 5 rows up yelled "come on" and then they tried harder.

A man and woman were on their first date.

"So, I hear you hunt deer," the woman said.

The man looked away and turned red.

"What's wrong?" asked the woman.

The man bashfully replied, "I'm not used to someone calling me 'dear' on the first date."

Q: Where do ghosts like to go swimming?
A: Lake Eerie.

The golfer stood over his tee shot for what seemed like an eternity, looking up, looking down, measuring the distance, and figuring the wind direction and speed. Generally, he was driving his partner nuts.

Finally, his exasperated partner said, "What is taking you so long? Hit the ball!"

"My wife is up there watching me from the clubhouse," the golfer answered. "I want to make this a perfect shot."

His partner pondered this for a moment, and then replied, "Forget it, you'll never hit her from here."

Q: What is a tree's least favorite month?
A: Sep-timber!

After winter, trees are re-leaved.

Q: What type of bread does a champion racehorse eat?

A: Thoroughbred.

Two windmills are standing in a field. One windmill asks, "What kind of music do you like?"

The other replies, "I'm a big metal fan."

Knock-knock!
Who's there?
Trigger.
Trigger who?
Trigger treat!

Q: What dance do cheesemakers do at Halloween?

A: The Muenster Mash.

Q: What happens when football players lose their eyesight?
A: They become referees.

Three guys are fishing in the Caribbean. One guy says, "I had a terrible fire and lost everything. Now the insurance company is paying for everything, and that's why I'm here."

The second guy says, "I had a terrible explosion. I lost everything. Now the insurance company is paying for everything, and that's why I'm here."

The third guy says, "What a coincidence! I had a terrible flood; I lost everything. Now the insurance company is paying for everything, and that's why I'm here!"

The other two guys turn to him with confusion and ask, "Flood? How do you start a flood?"

Q: What did March say to all the madness?
A: "What's all that bracket?"

At the nudist colony for Communists, two old men are sitting on the porch. One turns to the other and says, "I say, old boy, have you read Marx?"

And the other says, "Yes. I believe it's these wicker chairs."

Q: What's a runner's favorite subject in school?
A: Jog-graphy.

```
Why aren't you
in church?

-------------

Who are you to
judge?

-------------

God.

-------------

You shouldn't
text in church.
```

Two dimwitted golfers are teeing off on a foggy par-3. They can see the flag, but not the green. The first golfer hits his ball into the fog, and the second golfer does the same. Then they proceed to the green to find their balls.

One ball is about six feet from the cup, while the other had found its way into the cup for a hole-in-one. Both are playing the same brand of ball, and they can't figure out whose ball is whose.

They decide to ask the golf pro to weigh in. After congratulating both golfers on their fine shots, the golf pro asks, "Which one of you used the orange ball?"

@TheThryll

They should make a sequel to Groundhog Day, but it's the exact same movie.

Q: How is golf like taxes?
A: You drive hard to get to the green, and then you wind up in the hole.

Joel got home from his Sunday round of golf later than usual and very tired. "Bad day at the course?" his wife asked.

"Everything was going fine," he said. "Then Harry had a heart attack and died on the 10th tee."

"Oh, my," said his wife. "That's awful!"

"You're not kidding. For the whole back nine it was hit the ball, drag Harry, hit the ball, drag Harry…"

Q: What do gymnasts, acrobats, and bananas have in common?
A: They can all do the splits.

I went to buy camouflage trousers the other day. I couldn't find any.
—Tommy Cooper

Q: Why don't race car drivers eat before a big race?
A: They don't want to get Indy-gestion.

They called him the Crossword Puzzle boxer. He entered the ring vertical and left horizontal.

———————————

Two wrestlers are sitting on a park bench, and an old lady who's ranting and raving comes by.

"Hey!" she bellows in a hoarse voice. "I got a riddle for you two. What has two heads, four arms, four legs, and stinks something awful?"

The guys look at each other, and one of them shrugs. "I give up, what has two heads, four arms, four legs, and stinks something awful?"

"You and your friend!" The woman staggers away, chuckling.

The guys look at each other and start laughing. "That was a funny riddle that lady told us," they say. "Let's go try it on someone else."

Laughing hysterically, they see two guys. They approach them and smile. "Hey! We got a riddle for you! What has two heads, four arms, four legs, and stinks something awful?"

The guys shrug, waiting for the answer.

The wrestlers chuckle again, and one of them says with a smirk, "Me and my friend!"

Q: Why did the soccer player bring a string to the game?
A: So that she could tie the score.

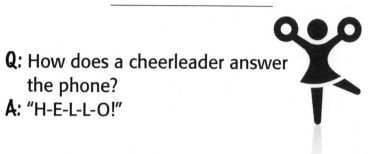

Q: How does a cheerleader answer the phone?
A: "H-E-L-L-O!"

American guy: Do you play video games?
French guy: Wii!

Q: Why don't grasshoppers go to football games?
A: They prefer cricket matches.

Q: What's a surfer's favorite detergent?
A: Tide.

Sherlock Holmes and Watson go camping. They hike out into the woods, find a clearing, and pitch their tent. They start a fire, roast marshmallows, drink a little, sing some campfire songs, and finally crawl into the tent and go to sleep.

Some hours later, Sherlock nudges Watson awake. "Watson!" he hisses. "Wake up! Tell me what you see."

Watson replies, "I see millions of stars. If just one out of every million of those stars has a planet and one out of every one of those million planets has life, then there must be millions of beings just like me out there, looking up at the same stars that I am and wondering the same questions."

"Watson, you fool!" Sherlock says. "Someone stole our tent!"

Q: What do surfing and oil have in common?
A: They're both measured by the barrel, brah.

Adin: What position does your brother play on the football team?
Jen: I think he's one of the drawbacks!

@ladybroseph

You win every marathon you don't run.

Q: What's green, smells like vinegar, and plays football?
A: The Green Bay Pickles.

A book fell on my head.
I only have my shelf to blame.

Q: When chickens go jogging, which way do they run?
A: Cluck-wise.

Two hunters charter a hydroplane to take them out into the wilderness. Once they land, the pilot tells them, "Okay, be back here same time next week for me to pick you up." The guys agree and depart on their trip.

The week rolls by, each man kills a moose, and they return to the dock to meet the plane. When the pilot sees their bounty, he says, "Hey, guys, I can't fit that all on the plane. We won't make it off the water!"

The guys look at each other, and one says, "Well, the last guy said that, too, but he took us." The pilot looks at his plane and the load again and begrudgingly agrees.

The plane struggles to get off the water. They're barely clearing the trees when *wham*! The plane sideswipes the side of a mountain. The plane crashes, but they never got very high off the ground to begin with, so they are all okay. They are also stranded. Lying out in the dirt, one says to the other, "Hey, Doug, where are we?"

Doug looks around and says, "Oh, 'bout a half a mile farther than we were last time."

Chuck Norris is so tough, he once delivered a roundhouse kick to the eye…of a hurricane. The result is now known as "widely scattered showers."

Only Chuck Norris can defeat a brick wall in a tennis match.

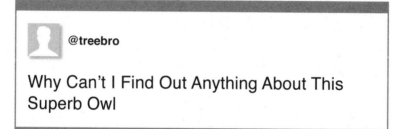

@treebro

Why Can't I Find Out Anything About This Superb Owl

Q: What happened when the monkey scored the winning goal?
A: The crowd went bananas.

Q: How did the monkey start a flea circus?
A: From scratch.

Q: Why can't horses dance?
A: Because they have two left feet.

_____

I watched a documentary about beavers last night. It was the best dam movie I've ever seen.

_____

Q: Where did the kittens go to see art?
A: A mew-seum.

A reporter meets a man carrying an eight-foot-long metal stick and asks, "Are you a pole vaulter?"

"No," says the man, "I'm German. But how did you know my name is Walter?"

Q: Why did Eric Clapton keep his guitar in the refrigerator?
A: So his songs would be cool.

Q: What kind of ice cream is bad at tennis?
A: Soft serve.

❝I'll tell you what I love doing more than anything: trying to pack myself in a small suitcase. I can hardly contain myself.❞
—TIM VINE

This guy goes to a costume party with a girl on his back.

"What are you supposed to be?" asks the host.

"I'm a snail," says the guy.

"But you have a girl on your back," replies the host.

"Yeah," he says, "that's Michelle."

_____

Q: Why did the dog cross the road twice?
A: He was trying to catch a boomerang.

_____

Q: Why did the angry Jedi cross the road?
A: To get to the Dark Side.

_____

If I buy a balloon at $0.99, how much should I sell it for, to account for inflation?

_____

Q: Why are penguin parties always
   so awkward?
A: They can't seem to break the ice.

I know how to start a fire using two pieces of wood. One has to be a matchstick.

Q: What time does Serena Williams wake up?
A: Ten-ish.

 @petebeatty

so what happens if the horse wins the triple crown? does he get to become human again at last? sorry i don't watch a lot of horsing racing

A man wanted a new hobby, so he bought a remote control airplane by mail order. To his surprise, it arrived in 189 pieces. The instructions said that it could be put together in an hour. All he wanted to do was fly his new plane! He worked and worked, frustrated and cursing, for two days. Finally, he had it assembled.

Feeling vengeful, he wrote a check for the plane, cut it into 189 pieces, and mailed it to the company.

Q: Why is basketball such a messy sport?
A: Because everybody dribbles on the floor.

A coach walks into the locker room before a game, looks over at his star player, and says, "I'm not supposed to let you play since you failed math, but we need you in there. So what I have to do is ask you a math question, and if you get it right, you can play."

The player agrees, and the coach looks into his eyes intently and asks, "Okay, now concentrate: What is two plus two?"

The player thinks for a moment and then answers, "Four?"

"Did you say four?!" the coach exclaims.

At that, all the other players on the team start yelling, "Come on, Coach, give him another chance!"

Q: Why does Santa have three gardens?
A: So he can hoe-hoe-hoe.

Q: What's the vampire's favorite part of a horse race?

A: When it's neck and neck.

I dreamed about drowning in an ocean of orange soda last night. It took me a while to realize it was just a Fanta sea.

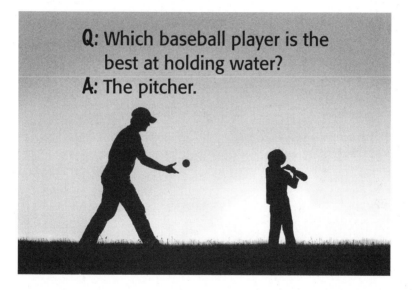

Q: Which baseball player is the best at holding water?

A: The pitcher.

Q: What do you get when you cross a pig and a frog?

A: A lifetime ban from the *Muppet Show* studio.

Q: What did the yogi say to the hot dog vendor?
A: "Make me one with everything."

I just read a lengthy book about Japanese sword fighters. I'll do my best to samurais it for you.

In high school football, the coach kept me on the bench all year. On the last game of the season, the crowd was yelling, 'We want Youngman! We want Youngman!' The coach finally says, 'Youngman, go see what they want!'

—Henny Youngman

Q: What's a balloon's least favorite genre of music?
A: Pop.

A psychology instructor had just finished a lecture on mental health and was giving an oral exam.

"How would you diagnose a patient who walks back and forth, screaming at the top of his lungs one minute, and then sits in a chair weeping uncontrollably the next?" she asked.

A young man raised his hand and answered, "A basketball coach?"

First golfer: Your trouble is that you're not addressing the ball correctly.
Second golfer: Yeah, well, I've been polite to the #$%& thing long enough.

Want to get noticed? Go jogging without moving your arms.

Q: Why does the stadium get so hot after a game?
A: All the fans leave.

Q: Why do golfers always carry two pairs of pants with them?
A: Just in case they get a hole in one.

———

Arnold Schwarzenegger is invited to a costume party. When asked what he'll dress up as, he says, "I'll be Bach."

———

"Help!" screamed the hunter into his cell phone. "I was trying to shoot a deer, and by mistake I killed my partner!"

"Okay," said the ranger into the phone, "try to calm yourself down. First I would like you to make *sure* he's dead."

"Okay," said the hunter. "Hold on one second." Suddenly, the ranger heard a *BANG!* The hunter came back on the line. "Okay, yeah, he's dead."

FOR YOUR HEALTH
Fitness, Aging, and Eventual Death

Man: My wife wants another baby, but do you think we should have kids after 40?
Doctor: No, 40 children is enough!

Q: What kind of exercise is perfect for lazy people?
A: Diddly squats!

Caller: Operator! Call me an ambulance!
Operator: Okay, you're an ambulance!

"When I was born I was so surprised, I didn't talk for a year and a half."

—Gracie Allen

Q: What's the difference between a primary care doctor and a specialist?
A: One treats what you have, the other thinks you have what he treats.

Q: Where do boats go when they get sick?
A: The dock.

Patient: When my hand heals, will I be able to play piano?
Doctor: Yes, you'll be fine in a few days.
Patient: Great! I've always wanted to play an instrument.

I wasn't planning to get a brain transplant, but then I changed my mind.

I do yoga two to three times a week. And by "doing yoga," I mean I put my foot in my mouth.

A New York doctor advised her patient to walk two miles a day. A month later the patient called and said, "I'm in Boston. What should I do now?"

I lost five pounds last week, but I found them in the fridge over the weekend.

A man woke up after a risky procedure. He shook his doctor's hand in gratitude and said, "I wouldn't want to insult you by offering you money. But I would like you to know that I've added you to my will."

"That's very kind of you," said the doctor. "Can I see that prescription I just gave you? I need to make a little change."

Migraines aren't real.
They're all in your head.

_____

Q: What do you call two doctors with colds?
A: An ironic paradox.

_____

My doctor advised me to stop having
intimate dinners for four unless
three other people are there.

_____

Nurse: Doctor, did you take the patient's
temperature?
Doctor: No, is it missing?

_____

Did you hear about the guy whose entire
left side was cut off? He's all right now.

_____

I have been diagnosed with a type of
amnesia where I can't remember
'80s bands. There is no Cure.

A lady went for a routine physical.

"Here," said the nurse, handing her a urine specimen cup. "The bathroom is to your right. The doctor will be with you shortly."

A few minutes later, the lady came out of the bathroom with an empty cup and a relieved look on her face.

"Thanks!" she said. "They had a toilet in there, so I didn't need this after all!"

Knock-knock!
Who's there?
Madison.
Madison who?
Time to take your Madison.

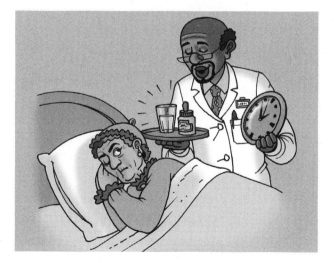

Two psychiatrists pass each other on the street.
   "You are fine. How am I?"

For years, an elderly gentleman could barely hear. Finally, he went to a doctor and was fitted for a set of hearing aids that fully restored his hearing. A month later, he had a checkup, and the doctor said, "Your hearing is perfect. Your family must be really pleased that you can hear again."
   "Oh, I haven't told them yet," the man replied. "I just sit around and listen to the conversations. I've changed my will three times!"

When I was a kid, I only had two friends. They were imaginary, and they would only play with each other.
—Ellen DeGeneres

I'm a walking economy. My hairline is in recession, my stomach is a victim of inflation, and it's all putting me into a deep depression.

Q: How can you identify a proctologist?
A: He's the doctor wearing a watch above
his elbow.

@thewritertype

They'll never win a war on drugs. It's hard
enough to win a war even when you're not
on drugs.

A young woman took her troubles to a
psychiatrist. "Doctor, you must help me,"
she pleaded. "It's gotten to the point that
every time I date a guy, I end up in bed with
him. And then afterward, I feel guilty and
depressed for a week."

"I see," nodded the psychiatrist. "And
you, no doubt, want me to strengthen your
willpower and resolve in this matter."

"No way!" exclaimed the woman. "I want
you to fix it so I won't feel guilty afterward."

Lying about my age is easier
now that I often forget what it is.

———————————

The other day I needed to pay a visit to a public restroom. It had two stalls. One of the doors was locked, so I went into the other one, closed the door, and sat down.

A voice came from the stall next to me: "Hey, how's it going?"

Although I thought that it was a bit strange, I didn't want to be rude, so I replied, "Not too bad, thanks."

Then I heard his voice again. "So, what are you up to?"

Again, I answered, somewhat reluctantly. "Just, you know, using the restroom. How about yourself?"

The next thing I heard him say was, "Sorry, I'll have to call you back. I've got some idiot in the stall next to me answering everything I say."

———————————

Knock-knock!
Who's there?
Venice.
Venice who?
Venice the last time I had a tetanus shot?

Four codgers were enjoying a cup of coffee at the local diner when one of them said, "Do you realize my hands hurt so much I can hardly hold this coffee cup?"

"Oh, that's nothing," said another. "My cataracts are so bad I can barely see my coffee cup."

"I got you two beat," said the third. "I've got arthritis and can't turn my head to the left or right."

"Aw, quit your complaining!" ordered the fourth. "At least we can still drive."

Doctor: How's that kid who swallowed the half-dollar?
Nurse: No change yet.

Somebody said that my father is older than dirt. It's not true—he discovered it.

_____

A hostess at a casino buffet showed a woman to her table.

"Could you keep an eye out for my husband?" the woman asked. "He has gray hair, wears glasses, has a potbelly—"

"Honey," she said, "today is Senior Day. They *all* look like that."

_____

Betty: I love your locket! Is there a memento inside?
Meg: Yes, a lock of my husband's hair.
Betty: But he's still alive.
Meg: True, but his hair is gone.

_____

You know you're getting old when you wake up with that morning-after feeling... and you didn't do anything the night before.

A little boy comes running into the room shouting, "Grandpa! Grandpa! Can you make a sound like a frog?"

"I don't know, why?" his grandpa replies.

"Because Grandma says we can go to Disneyland as soon as you croak!"

Recently I was told that I'm color-blind.
It came right out of the orange.

I used to have a fear of hurdles,
but I got over it.

A young lady saw an elderly couple sitting down to lunch at a fast-food restaurant. She noticed that they had ordered only one meal and an extra drink cup. As she watched, the gentleman carefully divided the hamburger in half. He counted out the fries, half for him, half for her. Then he poured half of the drink into the extra cup and set it in front of his wife. The old man then began to eat while his wife watched, with her hands folded in her lap.

The lady decided to buy another meal for them so that they didn't have to split theirs. She asked them first if it would be okay.

The old man said, "Oh, goodness, no. We've been married 60 years, and everything has always been and will always be shared, 50/50."

The lady then asked the wife if she was going to eat.

"Not yet," she said. "It's his turn with the teeth."

Gosh, I hope I get sick enough this year to justify the amount I spend on health insurance!

Q: What's brown and sounds like a bell?
A: Dung!

My wife says she's good at yoga.
I think she's a poser.

The mayor wanted to get more townspeople to attend the city council meetings. One council member suggested bringing in a hypnotist to do a show for everyone. They thought it was a great idea.

A few weeks later, the town hall was packed, and the people were fascinated as the hypnotist took out a pocket watch and began to chant, "Watch the watch, watch the watch, watch the watch..."

The crowd grew mesmerized as the watch swayed back and forth, back and forth, back and forth…

Suddenly the hypnotist's fingers slipped, and the watch fell to the floor. "Crap!" he said.

It took three weeks to clean up the town hall.

Have you heard about the new movie *Constipation*?

It hasn't come out yet.

There are three signs of old age. The first is memory loss. I forget the other two.

A man is in a public restroom, and he discovers there is no toilet paper. He calls to the next stall, "Do you have any toilet paper in there?"

"No," comes the reply.

"Do you have any newspaper?"

"Sorry!"

"Umm, do you have two fives for a ten?"

What's the difference between ignorance, apathy, and ambivalence?

I don't know and I don't care one way or the other.

A retired couple went to a doctor. The man said, "We want to know if we are making love properly. Will you look at us?"

"Go ahead," said the doctor. They made love in front of him. "You are doing it perfectly," the doctor said. "That will be $20."

They came back six weeks in a row and did the same thing. The doctor grew weary of seeing them. On the seventh visit, the doctor said, "Why are you here? I've already told you several times that you're fine!"

"She can't come to my retirement home," said the man, "and I can't go to hers. A motel costs $40. You charge us $20 and we get $15 back from Medicare."

The entire purpose of shinbones is so that we can find trailer hitches in the dark.

_____

Don't limp in here late with a lame excuse!

_____

Q: How many hyperactive kids does it take to screw in a light bulb?
A: Wanna go ride bikes?

_____

Once upon a time there were three sisters, aged 92, 94, and 96. They all lived together, and one night the 96-year-old ran a bath. She put one foot in and paused. "Was I getting in the tub or out?" she yelled.

The 94-year-old hollered back, "I don't know. I'll come and see." She started up the stairs and paused. "Was I going up or coming down?" she shouted.

The 92-year-old, sitting at the kitchen table having tea, overheard her sisters. She shook her head, said, "I sure hope I never get that forgetful," and knocked on the wood table for good measure. Then she yelled, "I'll come up and help both of you as soon as I see who's at the door!"

Sometimes I tuck my knees into my chest and lean forward. That's just how I roll.

Patient: Doctor, I keep thinking that I'm a deck of cards!
Psychiatrist: Sit over there. I'll deal with you later!

@scottsimpson

As I get older I like to take a little time every day to reflect on the course of my life and also shave my shoulders.

Lemar is out with his friends and stops by his grandmother's house for a visit. There's a bowl of peanuts on the coffee table, and Lemar and his friends start snacking on them.

Before they leave, his friends say, "Nice to meet you, ma'am, and thank you for the peanuts."

"You're welcome," Grandmother says. "Ever since I lost my dentures, all I can do is suck the chocolate off of them."

Q: Why can't you hear a pterodactyl in the bathroom?
A: Because the P is silent.

When people ask me if I exercise, I tell them I do crunches every day. Cap'n Crunch, Cinnamon Toast Crunch, Nestlé Crunch...

"I'm prescribing these pills for you," the doctor told her overweight patient, who tipped the scales at 350 pounds. "I don't want you to swallow them. Just spill them on the floor twice a day and pick them up, one at a time."

I think my favorite part of going to the gym is judging other people.

We're opening a gym called Resolutions. It will have exercise equipment for the first two weeks of the year and then turn into a bar for the rest of it.

Q: Why did the aerobics instructor cross the road?

A: Someone on the other side could still walk.

___

The word aerobics came about when the gym instructors got together and said, 'If we're going to charge $10 an hour, we can't call it jumping up and down.'

—Rita Rudner

___

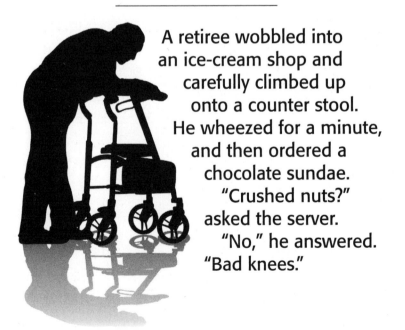

A retiree wobbled into an ice-cream shop and carefully climbed up onto a counter stool. He wheezed for a minute, and then ordered a chocolate sundae.

"Crushed nuts?" asked the server.

"No," he answered. "Bad knees."

There was an elderly couple who, in their old age, were getting forgetful. They decided to go to a doctor. The doctor told them that memory loss is a normal part of aging, but that they should start writing things down so they don't forget. They went home, and the woman asked her husband to get her a bowl of ice cream.

"You might want to write it down," she said.

"No, I can remember that you want a bowl of ice cream," he replied.

Then she told her husband she wanted whipped cream on it.

"Write it down," she told him, and again he said, "No, no, I can remember: you want a bowl of ice cream with whipped cream."

Then the woman said she wanted a cherry on top. "Write it down," she told her husband, and again he said, "No, I got it. You want a bowl of ice cream with whipped cream and a cherry on top."

He went to get the ice cream and spent an unusually long time in the kitchen. When he came out, he handed his wife a plate of eggs and bacon. His wife stared at the plate for a moment, then looked at her husband and asked, "Where's the toast?"

Q: Why did the blind lady fall into the well?
A: Because she couldn't see that well.

"Drinking removes warts and pimples. Not from me— from the people I look at."

—Jackie Gleason

I used to be addicted to the Hokey Pokey.
But then I turned myself around.

Q: What did the pirate say on his 80th birthday?
A: "Aye, matey."

Q: What happened to the pirate who couldn't pee?
A: He became irate.

Many people have decent hand-eye coordination. But pirates have good eye-eye coordination.

Grandpa's 100th birthday party was not a huge success. The family wheeled him in his chair out onto the lawn for a picnic. When he slowly started to lean to the right, his daughter stuffed a pillow on his right side to prop him up. A bit later, he started leaning to the left. His son straightened him up and stuffed a pillow on his left side. Soon he started tilting forward. This time his other son caught him and tied a pillow around his waist.

A few minutes later, his grandson arrived. He said, "Hey, Grandpa! How's life treating you?"

"Terrible," he said. "They won't let me fart."

Mary had a little lamb.
She's not a vegan anymore.

_____

Q: Why didn't anyone say anything when the king farted?
A: It was a noble gas.

@kellyoxford

Web MD is like a Choose Your Own Adventure book where the ending is always cancer.

Two old women are sitting on a bench waiting for a bus. "You know," one of the women says to the other, "I've been sitting here so long, my butt fell asleep."

The other woman turns to her and says, "I know! I heard it snoring!"

_____

Refusing to go to the gym counts as resistance training.

Patient: Doctor, my hair keeps falling out. What can you give me to keep it in?
Doctor: How about a shoebox?

A lady comes home from her doctor's appointment grinning from ear to ear. Her husband asks, "Why are you so happy?"

The wife says, "The doctor told me that for a 45-year-old woman, I have the breasts of an 18-year-old."

"Oh, really?" asks her husband. "What did he say about your 45-year-old a**?"

"Yeah, we didn't talk about you."

My doctor said he's been practicing for 25 years. I told him I'm not going back until he's ready to start doing it for real.

Q: What do you call a pony with a sore throat?
A: A little hoarse.

A man goes to a shrink and says, "Doctor, my wife is unfaithful to me. Every evening, she goes to the bar and picks up men. In fact, she sleeps with anybody who asks her! I'm going crazy. What do you think I should do?"

"Relax," says the doctor, "Take a deep breath and calm down. Now, tell me, exactly where is this bar?"

Two cows are standing in a field. One says to the other, "I got artificially inseminated today. Nine months from now I'll have a calf."

"I don't believe you," said the other cow.

"Really! No bull!"

A man working with an electric saw accidentally cuts off all of his fingers. At the emergency room, his doctor says, "Give me the fingers, and I'll see what I can do."

"But I don't have the fingers!" the injured man replies.

"Why didn't you bring them?" the doctor asks.

"How was I supposed to pick them up?"

Q: What do you call a man with six fingers?
A: Four fingers short.

Norma was driving to the store with her two friends in the backseat. At the first intersection, the light turned red and Norma powered right through it. Her friends were speechless. Norma ran the next red light as well. As they sailed through the third red light, one friend recovered herself and cried out, "Norma! We just ran three red lights! You're going to get us killed."

"Me?" Norma gasped. "I thought *you* were driving!"

I was going to buy a book about phobias, but I was afraid it wouldn't help me.

Q: Why did the library book go to the doctor?
A: It needed to be checked out. It had a bloated appendix.

Fresh out of the shower, a woman stood in front of the mirror complaining to her husband that her breasts were too small. Instead of telling her it's not true, he came up with a suggestion.

"If you want your breasts to grow, then every day take a piece of toilet paper and rub it between them for a few seconds."

Willing to try anything, she fetched a piece of toilet paper and stood in front of the mirror again, rubbing it between her breasts.

"How long will this take?" she asked.

"They'll grow larger over a period of years," her husband replied.

"Do you really think rubbing a piece of toilet paper between my breasts every day will make them larger?"

"It worked for your butt, didn't it?"

I'll never forget the last thing that Grandpa said before he kicked the bucket:
   "Hey, how far do you think I can kick this bucket?"

Q: What did the big bucket say to the small bucket?
A: "You're looking a little pail!"

I didn't like my mustache at first.
Then it grew on me.

"Doctor," a man says, "last night I had a Freudian slip. I was having dinner with my mother-in-law and wanted to say, 'Could you please pass the butter?' Instead, what came out was, 'You awful old crone, you've completely ruined my life!'"

An elderly gentleman went in for his annual physical exam.

"You're in incredible shape," the doctor said. "How old are you again?"

"I'm 78," the man replied.

"How do you stay so healthy? You look like a 60-year-old."

"Well, my wife and I made a pact when we got married that whenever she got mad she would go into the kitchen and cool off, and I would go outside to settle down."

"What does that have to do with it?" asked the doctor.

The man sighed. "I've pretty much lived an outdoor life."

Patient: Doctor, Doctor, you've got to help me!
Doctor: What's the trouble?
Patient: One night I dream that I'm a car's muffler. And then the next night, I dream that I'm part of the wheel.
Doctor: Why is that such a big deal?
Patient: I wake up exhausted and tired.

A healthy sleep not only makes your life longer, but also shortens the workday.

@M_Hedberg

I haven't slept for 10 days, because that would be too long.

As an old man stepped off a curb and started to cross the street, a car came screeching around the corner and headed straight for him. The alarmed man tried to hurry across the street, but the car changed lanes and maintained its collision course. So the man turned around and started to cross back to the curb, but the car switched lanes again. Panicking, the man froze in the middle of the road. The car pulled up beside him, and the window rolled down. The driver was a squirrel.

"See?" said the squirrel. "It's not as easy as it looks."

Q: What is Beethoven doing in his grave?
A: Decomposing.

If you bury someone in the wrong place, you've made a grave mistake.

I saw an ad for burial plots and thought to myself, *This is the last thing I need.*

Q: Why did the hipster burn his tongue?
A: He drank his coffee before it was cool.

Conjunctivitis.com—
now that's a site for sore eyes.

Did you hear about the funeral for boiled water?
It was mist.

John stood before the Pearly Gates, and St. Peter asked him, "Have you done anything in your life that would qualify you to enter heaven?"

"Well, there's one thing. On a trip to South Dakota, I came upon a gang of bikers who were threatening an old lady. I told them to leave her alone, but they wouldn't listen. So I went right up to the biggest, most heavily tattooed biker. I whacked him on the head, kicked his bike over, ripped out his nose ring, threw it on the ground, and told him 'Leave her alone now, or you'll answer to me!'"

St. Peter was impressed. "When did his happen?"

"Just a couple minutes ago."

Q: How many optometrists does it take to change a light bulb?
A: 1 or 2. 1...or 2?

Q: What's red and bad for your teeth?
A: A brick.

66Want to wake up with a smile on your face? Go to sleep with a clothes hanger in your mouth.99
—Totie Fields

A receptionist said to the psychiatrist, "A man is out here who says he is invisible."

The doctor replied, "Tell him I can't see him right now."

Did you hear about the Buddhist who refused novocaine during his root canal?

He wanted to transcend dental medication.

Q: Why did the muffin go to the doctor?
A: He was feeling crummy.

An old geezer says to his buddy, "I hear you're getting married."

"Yes, I am!"

"Have I met her?"

"Nope!"

"Is she good-looking?"

"Not especially."

"Can she cook?"

"Not really."

"Is she loaded?"

"Poor as a church mouse."

"Well, then, why do you want to marry her?"

"She still drives!"

@billmurray

What if soymilk is just regular milk introducing itself in Spanish?

My doctor told me to cut down on my sodium. But I always take her advice with a grain of salt.

Knock-knock!
Who's there?
Uphill.
Uphill who?
Uphill would make me feel better.

Patient: Doctor, I think I need glasses.
Teller: You certainly do! This is a bank.

A guy goes to a psychiatrist. "Doctor, I keep having these alternating recurring dreams. First, I'm a teepee; then I'm a wigwam; then I'm a teepee; then I'm a wigwam. It's driving me crazy. What's wrong with me?"

The doctor replies: "It's very simple. You're two tents."

Q: Why couldn't the toilet paper cross the road?
A: Because it got stuck in a crack.

Four out of five people suffer from diarrhea.
Which means one enjoys it.

Q: What does a vegan zombie say?
A: "Graaains! Graaaains!"

The reading of a will is a dead giveaway.

Q: How can you tell when a mummy has a cold?
A: He starts coffin.

My six-pack is very precious to me. That's why I protect it with a layer of fat.

Patient: Doc, I don't believe that peanuts are fattening.
Doctor: Well, have you ever seen a skinny elephant?

Q: What did the doctor say to the patient after the operation was finished?
A: "That's enough out of you!"

@dril

If your grave doesn't say "rest in peace" on it you are automatically drafted into the skeleton war.

A man told his doctor that he wasn't able to do all the things around the house that he used to do. When the examination was complete, he said, "Now, Doc, I can take it. Tell me in plain English what is wrong with me."

"In plain English," the doctor replied, "you're just really lazy."

"Okay," said the man. "Now give me the medical term so I can tell my wife."

Having a 12-inch nose is anatomically
impossible, because at that point
it becomes a foot.

Q: Why was the farmer arrested at the gym?
A: He was destroying his calves.

What did the daddy chimney say to the
baby chimney?
"You're too little to smoke!"

The biggest loser at my weight-loss club was
an elderly woman.
"How'd you do it?" another club member
asked.
"Easy," she said. "Every night I take my teeth
out at six o'clock."

The advantage of exercising every day is so
when you die, everyone will say, "Well, she
looks good, doesn't she!"

Q: How many bodybuilders does it take to screw in a light bulb?
A: Three. One to do it and two to tell him, "You're looking huge man, you're looking huge!"

Q: What did the bodybuilder say when he opened his tub of protein powder?
A: "No whey!"

Did you hear about the weightlifter who got kicked out of his house? He was squatting.

I opened a gym geared towards lazy pessimists. It didn't work out.

The Upside of Old Age

- There's nothing left anymore to learn the hard way.
- Things that you buy now won't wear out.
- You no longer think of the speed limit as a challenge.
- Your investment in health insurance is finally paying off.
- Kidnappers are not very interested in you.
- You can quit trying to hold in your stomach no matter who walks into the room.
- Your secrets are safe with your friends because people your age can't remember them anyway.

My doctor told me to avoid stress, so I'm choosing to not open her bill.

Q: How do you hide money from a surgeon?
A: Tape it to his kids.

___

Did you hear the joke about germs?
Never mind, I don't want to spread it around.

___

I get plenty of exercise: jumping to conclusions, pushing my luck, and dodging responsibility.

___

Q: Why did the banana go to the doctor?
A: It wasn't peeling well.

___

Q: How many psychologists does it take to change a light bulb?
A: Just one, but the light bulb has to *want* to change.

Neurotics build castles in the sky.
Psychopaths live in them.
Psychiatrists collect the rent.

———————

Q: Where do hippos go to college?
A: Hippocampus.

———————

What did the hippocampus say when
it retired?
    "Thanks for the memories."

———————

The psychiatrist said to the cannibal at the
end of a session, "Your problem is simple.
You're just fed up with people."

———————

Going vegetarian is a missed steak.

———————

Q: What did the left eye say to the right eye?
A: "Between you and me, something smells."

A snowman sniffs and says, "I smell carrots."

Someone stole my mood ring.
I don't know how I feel about that.

Knock-knock!
Who's there?
Cologne.
Cologne who?
Cologne Ranger!

Did you hear that the maker of
spaghetti died? He pasta way.

Q: How many narcissists does it take to change a light bulb?
A: Just one. All he has to do is hold it in place while the world revolves around him.

At 20 we worry about what others think of us. At 40 we don't care about what others think of us. At 60 we discover they haven't been thinking about us at all.

—Ann Landers

Patient: Doc, I can't stop singing "What's New Pussycat?"
Therapist: Hmm, that sounds like Tom Jones syndrome.
Patient: Is it common?
Therapist: It's not unusual.

I'm not old, I'm in energy-saving mode.

Q: What kind of food should you eat to
increase your vision?
A: Seafood.

_____

Sarah loves wheat—wheat bread, wheat rolls,
wheat muffins—she can't get enough wheat.
The only problem is that she's quite allergic
to it. Whenever she eats it, she breaks out in a
rash. But does that ever stop her? Nope. She's
a real gluten for punishment.

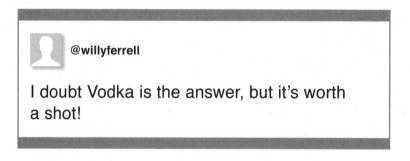

@willyferrell

I doubt Vodka is the answer, but it's worth
a shot!

Q: How do you kill a vampire from Texas?
A: With a chicken-fried stake.

_____

Hospitals are the only place where "positive"
means something bad, and "negative" is good.
When I hear test results, I say, "Oh, no! Or yay!
Which is it?"

The psychiatrist tells his patient, "I think you're crazy."

"I want a second opinion," his patient replies.

The psychiatrist says, "Okay, you're ugly, too!"

———

A Freudian slip is when you say one thing and mean your mother.

———

"Doc, did you run my health insurance?"

"Laughter is the best medicine, but your plan only covers chuckles and chortles."

———

Hold on, I have something in my shoe. Although I'm *pretty* sure it's a foot.

———

Patient: Doctor, no matter where I go or what I do, people just seem to ignore me.
Doctor: Next!

A veterinarian felt ill and went to see her doctor. The doctor was asking all the usual questions about symptoms and how long they had been occurring, when the vet interrupted him. "Hey, look, I'm a veterinarian. I don't need to ask my patients these kinds of questions. I can tell what's wrong just by looking. Why can't you?"

The doctor nodded, looked her up and down, wrote out a prescription, and handed it to her. He said, "There you go. Of course, if that doesn't work, we'll have to put you down."

_____

Q: Why didn't the cyclist win the race?
A: He just wasn't pumped enough.

_____

Q: If you're American when you go into the bathroom and American when you come out, what are you when you're *in* the bathroom?
A: European.

England doesn't have a kidney bank.
It does, however, have a Liverpool.

@bobvulfov

COP: u were swerving a lot so i have to
conduct a sobriety test
ME: ok
COP: lets get taco bell
ME: no
COP: text your ex
ME: no
COP: ok ur good

A highway patrol officer tried to pull over
a speeding car on the interstate, but the
car wouldn't stop. He pulled alongside the
car and was astounded to see that the old
woman behind the wheel was knitting,
completely oblivious to the patrol car's
flashing lights and siren. The officer shouted
over his loudspeaker, "Pull over!"

"No," the old lady yelled back, "it's a scarf!"

Q: What do you call someone who never farts in public?
A: A private tutor.

```
Mom wants you to
get her prego.
-------------
Well I can't. I
had that problem
solved years
ago.
-------------
What?? OMG DAD!!
TMI! Gross! Mom
wants PREGO
pasta sauce!
-------------
Oh, ok.
```

Smile and the world smiles with you.
Fart and the world suddenly stops smiling.

Q: What is the definition of "surprise"?
A: A fart with a lump in it!

An elderly couple is in church. The wife leans over and whispers to her husband, "I just let out a long, silent fart. What should I do?"

The husband replies, "First off, replace the batteries in your hearing aid."

_____

A woman went to see a therapist because she was troubled that she didn't have any friends.

The therapist asked, "What do you think might be causing the problem?"

The woman replied, "That's what I'm paying *you* to tell me! What, are you so lazy you want me to do your job for you? If I knew already, I wouldn't be here, would I—you fat, ugly jerk!"

_____

" *A man says, 'Doc, I gotta strawberry growing out of my head!' The doc says, 'Here's some cream to put on it.'* "

—Tommy Cooper

_____

My therapist says I have a preoccupation with vengeance. We'll see about that.

Q: What has a bottom at the top?
A: Your legs.

_____

Q: What are the directions to a urologist's office?
A: Follow the yellow brick road.

_____

Two old guys were sitting under a tree, watching the sun go down. One says, "You know, I'm 84, and my body is full of aches and pains. You're about my age. How do you feel?"

The other guy says, "Oh, I feel like a newborn baby."

"Really?" asks the first guy.

"Yep," says the second one. "No teeth, no hair, and I think I just wet my pants."

_____

Q: When does a cup of tea cause a stabbing pain in the eye?
A: When you forget to take out the spoon.

Claustrophobic people are more productive thinking outside of the box.

When an employment application asks who is to be notified in case of emergency, I always write, "A very good doctor."

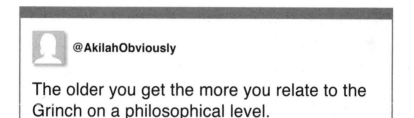

@AkilahObviously

The older you get the more you relate to the Grinch on a philosophical level.

Q: What did the teddy bear say when he was offered dessert?
A: "No thanks, I'm stuffed!"

A pessimist's blood type is always B-negative.

Three guys are fishing when an angel appears.

The first guy says, "I've suffered from back pain for years. Can you help me?"

The angel touches the man's back, and he feels instant relief.

The second guy points to his thick glasses and begs for a cure for his poor eyesight. When the angel tosses the lenses into the lake, the man gains 20/20 vision.

As the angel turns to the third fellow, the man instantly recoils and screams, "Don't touch me! I'm on disability!"

Q: What do you get when you cross a dyslexic, an insomniac, and an agnostic?

A: Someone who lies awake at night wondering if there is a dog.

Q: Why did the kid have string beans stuck up his nose?
A: He wasn't eating right.

_____

Q: Why didn't the kid wash his neck?
A: He wanted it to match his hands.

_____

A proctologist is walking around his office with a rectal thermometer tucked behind his ear. He goes into a staff meeting to discuss the day's activities, and a coworker asks why he has a thermometer behind his ear. In a wild motion he grabs for the thermometer, looks at it, and shouts, "Then where did I put my pen?"

_____

My wife left me because of my obsessive-compulsive issues. I told her to close the door five times on the way out.

A resident at a retirement community turned 100 years old, and the staff threw him a big birthday party. Even his son showed up.

"How old are you?" a tenant asked the son.

"I'm 81 years old," he answered.

The tenant shook her head. "They sure grow up fast, don't they?"

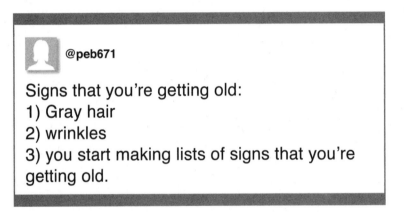

@peb671

Signs that you're getting old:
1) Gray hair
2) wrinkles
3) you start making lists of signs that you're getting old.

You know you're getting old when your joints become more accurate than the National Weather Service.

Q: What do old people call happy hour?
A: Nap time.

Did you hear the one about the 83-year-old woman who talked herself out of a speeding ticket?

She told the officer that she had to get somewhere before she forgot where she was going.

A man had never had surgery before, and he was waiting in the hospital nervously.

"This is a very simple, noninvasive procedure," the anesthesiologist reassured him.

"That makes me feel a little better."

"Heck," the doctor continued, "you have a better chance of dying from the anesthesia than the surgery itself."

An undertaker calls a man, 'About your mother-in-law, should we embalm her, cremate her, or bury her?' He says, 'Do all three. Don't take any chances.'

—Myron Cohen

Texting Abbreviations for Seniors

BFF: Best Friend Fainted
BYOT: Bring Your Own Teeth
CBM: Covered by Medicare
FWB: Friend with Beta-blockers
LMDO: Laughing My Dentures Out
GGPBL: Gotta Go, Pacemaker Battery Low!

Two elderly ladies had been friends since they were in their 30s. Now well into their 80s, they still got together a couple of times a week to play cards. One day, they were playing gin rummy, and one of them said, "You know, we've been friends for many years and, please don't get mad, but for the life of me, I can't remember your name. Please tell me what it is."

Her friend glared at her. She continued to stare at her for at least three minutes. Finally, she said, "How soon do you need to know?"

My doctor told me that jogging
could add years to my life. He was right—
I feel ten years older already.

Every night after work, a doctor named Richard stopped off at a bar for a chicory daiquiri. The bartender would always have the drink waiting at precisely 5:01 p.m.

One afternoon, as five o'clock approached, the bartender noticed that he was completely out of chicory. Improvising, he concocted a daiquiri made with hickory nuts and set it on the bar. The doctor came in at 5:01 p.m., took one sip of the drink, and exclaimed, "This isn't a chicory daiquiri!"

"No," replied the bartender, "It's not a chicory daiquiri, Dick. It's a hickory daiquiri, Doc."

"Why does your sister jump up and down before taking her medicine?"

"Because the label says to shake well before using!"

I'm mad! A couple years ago my therapist told me I had problems letting go of the past.

Q: How can you tell if a woman is wearing panty hose?
A: If she farts, her ankles swell.

The Upside of Old Age, Part II

- You can sing along with elevator music.
- Your eyes won't get too much worse.
- People don't call you past 8:00 p.m. anymore.
- You can eat dinner at 4:00 in the afternoon.
- In a hostage situation, you're the most likely to be released first.
- No one expects you to run— anywhere.
- You are no longer viewed as a hypochondriac.

A man goes to the doctor and says, "Doctor, wherever I touch, it hurts."

"What do you mean?" the doctor asks.

"When I touch my shoulder, it hurts. If I touch my knee…*ouch*! When I touch my forehead, it really, *really* hurts."

"I know what's wrong with you," the doctor says. "You've broken your finger!"

Knock-knock!
Who's there?
Abby.
Abby who?
Yow! Abby stung me.

A plumber attended to a leaking faucet at a neurosurgeon's house. After a two-minute job, he demanded $150. The neurosurgeon exclaimed, "I don't even charge that much, and I'm a brain surgeon."

The plumber replied, "You're right! I didn't either, when I was a surgeon. That's why I switched to plumbing."

Patient: Doctor, my stomach is getting really big.
Doctor: You should diet.
Patient: What color?

A friend used to be addicted to drinking detergent. But he's clean now.

Dear Santa,

Next Christmas all I want is a fat bank account and a slim body. Let's try not to mix up the two like you did last year, okay?

A guy bursts into a psychiatrist's office. "Doc!" he says, "I have suicidal tendencies! What should I do?"
"Pay me in advance."

A psychiatrist had to have a talk with his receptionist. "Just say that we're very busy," he said. "Please stop telling people that 'it's a madhouse.'"

I'm 83, and I feel like a 20-year-old, but unfortunately there's never one around.

—Milton Berle

An engineer and a psychiatrist meet up for their 20th college reunion. The engineer says, "I'm surprised to see you still looking so young. I'd have thought listening to people's problems all day would have given you a mass of wrinkles."

The psychiatrist replies, "You think we listen?"

At my age, I don't need health food. The more preservatives I can get, the better!

Father: Doctor, please hurry. My son swallowed a razor blade.
Doctor: Don't panic, I'm coming immediately. Have you done anything yet?
Father: Yeah, I shaved with the electric razor.

Any salad can be a Caesar...
if you stab it enough.

Never go to a doctor whose office plants have died.

—Erma Bombeck

A guy walks into a doctor's office. There's a banana stuck in one of his ears, a cucumber in the other ear, and a carrot in one nostril. "Doc, this is terrible. What's wrong with me?" he asks.

The doctor says, "Well, first of all, you need to eat more sensibly."

A cop pulls over a vehicle on the freeway. There are three little old ladies in the car.

"Why were you driving only 20 miles per hour?" he asks the driver.

"I was just going the posted speed limit!" She points to a sign up ahead.

The officer corrects her. "That's not the speed limit sign, that's the sign for this highway—Route 20!"

"We tried to tell you, Sheila!" says one of the passengers.

The cop takes another look at the old women and sees that they are wide-eyed and disheveled. One of them is tightly gripping the door handle, white-knuckled.

"What's the matter?" the cop asks.

"We just came off of Interstate 120."

If we aren't supposed to have midnight snacks, then why is there a light in the fridge?

Seven-year-old girl: A boy in my class asked me to play doctor.
Mother: Oh, dear. What happened?
Girl: Nothing! He made me wait 45 minutes and then double-billed the insurance company.

If vegetarians eat vegetables,
what do humanitarians eat?

_____

Q: Why did the pie go to the dentist?
A: It needed a filling.

Have you ever tried to seduce a sweet tooth?
It's a piece of cake!

Q: What do you call a bear with no teeth?
A: A gummy bear.

An elderly Florida man was driving down I-95.
  "Frank. Frank! Be careful," his wife shouted.
"I just heard on the radio that there's a car
going the wrong way down I-95!"
  "It's not just one car!" Frank yelled back.
"There are hundreds of them!"

When the actress saw her first strands
of gray hair, she thought she'd dye.

Went to see a doctor today who told me I had
four months to live. So I shot him. The judge
sentenced me to 20 years. Much better.

Old Matt: Windy today.
Old Jim: No, It's Thursday.
Old Bob: So am I. Let's go get a milkshake.

It's rare to get good cell reception
at a cemetery. It's a dead zone.

> **@abbycohenwl**
>
> By the time I get used to how old I am, I'm
> 10 years older than that.

Driving past a cemetery:
Dad: I wouldn't want to be buried in
this graveyard.
Kid: Why not?
Dad: Because I'm not dead yet!

You know you're getting older when, after they light the candles on the birthday cake, you pass out from heat exhaustion.

"I've got a great doctor. If you can't afford the operation, he touches up your X-rays."

—Henny Youngman

Doctor: I have some bad news and some very bad news.
Patient: Well, might as well give me the bad news first.
Doctor: The lab called with your test results. They said you have 24 hours to live.
Patient: 24 hours! That's terrible! What could be worse? What's the very bad news?
Doctor: I've been trying to reach you since yesterday.

YOU CAN'T MAKE THIS STUFF UP
Real-life Funnies

From a real court transcript:

Q: Well, sir, judging from your answer on how you reacted to the emergency call, it sounds like you are a man of intelligence and good judgment.

A: Thank you, and if I weren't under oath, I would return the compliment.

Accidentally Funny Newspaper Headlines

REASON FOR MORE BEAR SIGHTINGS:
MORE BEARS

Sᴛᴀᴛᴇ Sᴀʏs Cᴏsᴛ ᴏғ Sᴀᴠɪɴɢ Mᴏɴᴇʏ Tᴏᴏ Hɪɢʜ

New housing for elderly not yet dead

Death Is Nation's Top Killer

**Mayor Says D.C. Is Safe
Except for Murders**

A REASON FOR ODOR FOUND
AT SEWER PLANT

Sign at a railroad station:
"Beware! To touch these wires is instant death.
Anyone found doing so will be prosecuted."

_____

A town called Ugley in England is home to a civic group called the Ugley Women's Institute. They meet every month for scholarly lectures and afternoon tea. After being the butt of jokes for years, members finally renamed it the Women's Institute of Ugley. Still, when they identify their affiliation at conventions, they wind up announcing: "We're Ugley."

_____

Messages Seen on Church Reader Boards

"Do not criticize your wife's judgment—
see who she married"

"There's no A/C in Hell either"

"God shows no favoritism but our sign guy does. Go Cubs!"

"Swallowing pride will never give you indigestion"

"Life stinks. We have a pew for you"

Passive-Aggressive Office Notes… and Responses

ALL REFRIGERATORS WILL BE CLEANED OUT EVERY FRIDAY EFFECTIVE IMMEDIATELY.

Or when I am hungry

Please check your food — something has died in here, Thanks

Fluffy? Oh no! Not Fluffy! Wahhh!

It can't be Fluffy. He died in the other fridge.

3 scoops of grounds brews a great pot of coffee.

If you like coffee so weak that you can see through it

If you're looking for MUD please see Starbucks :)

Considering that Starbucks is one of the most successful businesses in history, they probably know a thing or two about making coffee.

Funny Couple Names from Newspaper Wedding Announcements

Kara Gorey + John Butcher = Gorey-Butcher

Elizabeth House + Christopher Reckker = House-Reckker

Annette King + Brian Sizer = King-Sizer

Crystal Butts + Levi McCracken = Butts-McCracken

Michael Greene + Sarah Flem = Greene-Flem

Paul Flynt + Loural Stone = Flynt-Stone

@bananafitz

ITEMS EVERY WOMAN SHOULD OWN:
-Little Black Dress
-Cute flats
-Strappy s- ok now that the men have stopped reading, we revolt at dawn.

At Least You're Better Than the Worst Movie Dads, ranked by *Salon Magazine*

1. John Milton, *The Devil's Advocate*; 2. Darth Vader, *Stars Wars*; 3. Noah Cross, *Chinatown*; 4. Grandpa, *The Texas Chainsaw Massacre*

From a real court transcript:
Q: Doctor, as a result of your examination of the plaintiff, is the young lady pregnant?
A: The young lady is pregnant, but not as a result of my examination.

Real Thank-You Note from a Kid
"Dear Mom,
Thank you for taking good care of me.
I hope you do better things for me."

Real Quips from Flight Attendants

• "At the pointy end of the plane is our captain."

• "We'll be coming through the cabin to make sure your seat belts are fastened and your shoes match your outfit."

• "In the event of a sudden loss of cabin pressure, oxygen masks will descend from  the ceiling. Stop screaming, grab the mask, and pull it over your face. If you have a small child traveling with you, secure your mask before assisting with theirs. If you are traveling with two small children, decide now which one you love more."

❝I gave my father $100 and said, 'Buy yourself something that will make your life easier.' So he went out and bought a present for my mother.❞

—Rita Rudner

Lunch Box Note Written By Parent
"The croutons go on your salad. NOT in your pants."

More Accidentally Funny Headlines

STUDY FINDS SEX, PREGNANCY LINK

Panda Mating Fails, Veterinarian Takes Over

Nude Scene Done Tastefully in Radio Play

Astronaut Welcomes Baby from Space

Breast Augmentation Available at Moundview

SOVIET VIRGIN LANDS SHORT OF GOAL AGAIN

Clever "Men" and "Women" Restroom Door Signs

"Nuts" and "No Nuts"

"Marios" and "Princess Toadstools"

"For Those Who Stand" and "For Those Who Sit"

"Pointers" and "Setters"

"Stouts" and "Lagers"

"The Ladies' Room is across the hall" and "The Men's Room is across the hall"

Sign in a department store:
"Bargain Basement Upstairs"

A French ambassador, M. Cambon, once thanked a Chicago mayor for a tour of the city. "Thank you," he said. "But I am sorry so to cockroach on your time."

The mayor replied, "You don't mean 'cockroach'; it is 'encroach' you mean."

"Oh, is it?" Cambon asked. "I see, a difference in gender."

Robin's Outbursts from the '60s *Batman* TV Show

"Holy taxidermy, Batman!"

"Holy bank balance, Batman!"

"Holy rats in a trap, Batman!"

"Holy squirrel cage, Batman!"

"Holy contributing to the delinquency of minors, Batman!"

"Holy hole in a doughnut, Batman!"

Real Thank-You Note from a Kid
"Dear Grandma and Grandpa,
Thanks for what you got me.
P.S. I forgot what you got me."

Names of Real Law Firms
Gunn & Hicks (Mississippi)
Dumas & McPhail (Alabama)
Bull & Lifshitz (New York)
Payne & Fears (California)
Jeep & Blazer (Illinois)
Lawless & Lawless (California)

Real Road Names
Old Guy Road (Damon, TX)
Tater Peeler Road (Lebanon, TN)
Unexpected Road (Buena, NJ)
Divorce Court (Heather Highlands, PA)
Psycho Path (Traverse City, MI)

In 1940 the *Washington Post* ran this headline about President Franklin Delano Roosevelt: "FDR IN BED WITH COED." He was actually in bed…with a cold.

"I always wanted to be somebody, but now I realize I should have been more specific."

—Lily Tomlin

From a real call to tech support:
Tech: Okay ma'am, do you see the button on the right-hand side of your mouse?
Caller: No, there's a printer and a phone on the right-hand side of my mouse.

Sign outside a photographer's studio:
"Have the kids shot for Dad from $24.95."

@SamGrittner

Saw a guy with three lip-ring piercings on the subway today. Took everything in my power not to attach a shower curtain.

Real Court Case Names
- *Batman v. Commissioner*
- *United States v. Forty Barrels and Twenty Kegs of Coca-Cola*
- *The California Coalition of Undressed Performers v. Spearmint Rhino*
- *United States v. Forty-three Gallons of Whisky*
- *Easter Seals Society for Crippled Children v. Playboy Enterprises*
- *One 1958 Plymouth Sedan v. Pennsylvania*
- *United States v. 12 200-Foot Reels of Super 8mm Film*
- *Death v. Graves*

From a real court transcript:
Defense: Your Honor, I have a short witness.
Judge: How short?
Defense: It's Mr. Long.
Judge: Put Long on.
Prosecutor: As long as he's short.

Real Band Names
- Japancakes
- Alcoholocaust
- Furious George
- JFKFC
- The Dictatortots
- Hostile Comb-Over
- Kathleen Turner Overdrive
- Harmonica Lewinsky
- Mary Tyler Morphine
- Ringo Deathstarr

(B)Ad Campaign
Cue Toothpaste was marketed in France by Colgate-Palmolive until they learned that *Cue* is also the name of a popular pornographic magazine in that country.

Sign on a community center in Pennsylvania:
"Auction Sunday—New and Used Food"

Real Bathroom Graffiti
- THE WORLD IS FLAT—Class of 1492
- ᴛᴏʟᴋɪᴇɴ ɪꜱ ʜᴏʙʙɪᴛ-ꜰᴏʀᴍɪɴɢ.
- We've been having a bad spell of wether.
- *Laugh and the world laughs with you. Snore and you sleep alone.*

Carly Houston was arrested for disorderly conduct in 2010. At the station, she used her one phone call to dial…911. "I'm trapped!" she said. "You gotta get someone in here to get me out of here!" One more charge was added: making a false emergency call.

Actual Restaurant Names
- Just for the Halibut
- Pony Espresso
- Lawrence of Oregano
- Wiener Take All
- Relish the Thought
- Syriandipity
- Jonathan Livingston Seafood
- Boogie Woogie Bagel Boy
- Brew Ha Ha
- Adams Rib
- Barnum and Bagel

Real People's Names and Professions
Sue Yoo, lawyer
Gunnar Stickler, pediatrician
Les McBurney, firefighter
Larry Sprinkle, weather forecaster
Paul Paulos, St. Paul police sergeant
Robin Mahfood, CEO of Food for the Poor

@meganamram

There's literally no way to know how many chameleons are in your house

Actual Music Genres
Cute Metal: Japanese pop music meets metal, performed by and for kids.

Nintendocore: A dissonant blend of hard rock and video game music...plus screaming.

Chap Hop: Britain's version of gangster rap, if gangsters were actually sophisticated dandies who sing about wearing tweed and drinking tea.

Accidentally Funny Political Headlines

RED TAPE HOLDS UP NEW BRIDGE

William Kelly Was Fed Secretary

Joint Chiefs Head Will Be Replaced

*Hearings to Be Held on
Statue of Liberty's Crown*

2 States May See Delegates Halved

Hand Waves Goodbye to County Board

From a real court transcript:
Q: Do you drink alcohol?
A: No, sir.
Q: Are you a teetotaler?
A: Not really. Just coffee once in a while.

Real Villages in the United Kingdom

Foulbog	Limpley Stoke
Slaggyford	Moss of Barmuckity
Corney	Nempnett Thrubwell
Nether Wallop	Belchford

More Law Firm Names
Low, Ball & Lynch (California)
Smart & Biggar (Toronto)
Bickers & Bickers (Pennsylvania)
Pope & Gentile (California)
Boring & Coy (Indiana)
Angst & Angst (Pennsylvania)
Lies & Bullis (North Dakota)

Sign next to a red traffic light:
"This light never turns green"

A real call to tech support:
Caller: Now what do I do?
Tech: What is the prompt on the screen?
Caller: It's asking for "Enter Your Last Name."
Tech: Okay, so type in your last name.
Caller: How do you spell that?

Real Thank-You Note from a Kid
"Thank you for the amazing squirt gun I
will shoot you with."

More Passive-Aggressive Office Notes... and Responses

DON'T put dishes in the sink. Wash it or put it in the dishwasher...

If the dishwasher is full empty it!!!! Your mom does not live here.

She lives in Phoenix now, with her new boyfriend Jerry. All because you wouldn't do your dishes.

If I'm not here, please check reception

You weren't there either... :(

Where are you?????

We miss you.

0 DAYS WITHOUT SACARSM

Nice spelling!!

The printer is here temporarily

In the greater scheme of things, aren't we all?

From a real court transcript:
Q: Doctor, how many autopsies have you performed on dead people?
A: All my autopsies have been on dead people.

Sign in an office building:
"Toilet out of order. Please use floor below."

"American" Products Around the World

• In Spain, duct tape is called *cinta americana*, or American tape.

• In France, brass knuckles are *le poing américan*, or the American fist.

• In Brazil, iceberg lettuce is *alface americana*, which is American lettuce.

• In Slovenia, coleslaw is *amerika solate*, or American salad.

• In Japan, a corn dog is an *amerikandoggu*.

• In Italy, a placemat is *tovaglietta all-americana*, or a little American tablecloth.

More Accidentally Funny Headlines

COMPLAINTS ABOUT NBA REFEREES
GROWING UGLY

U.S. Ships Head to Somalia

Fried Chicken Cooked in Microwave Wins Trip

**Textron Inc. makes offer to screw
company stockholders**

Factory Orders Dip

MINUS SHORTS, BANKS GET BREATHING ROOM

Teen Learns to Live With Stutttering

DEAD EXPECTED TO RISE

Looney Laws

- It's against the law in Oklahoma to display a hypnotized person in a window.

- It's illegal in Washington State to pretend that your parents are rich.

- In Florida, widows may not skydive on Sundays.

- By law, Washington drivers must carry an anchor to be used as an emergency brake.

A group of non-English speakers chose "diarrhea" as one of the prettiest-sounding English words.

More Quips from Flight Attendants

• "Welcome to Amarillo. Please remain in your seats with your seat belts fastened while the captain taxis what's left of our airplane to the gate."

• "Ladies and gentlemen, if you wish to smoke, the smoking section on this airplane is on the wing. If you can light 'em, you can smoke 'em."

• "This aircraft is equipped with a video surveillance system that monitors the cabin during taxiing. Any passengers not remaining in their seats until the aircraft comes to a full and complete stop at the gate will be strip-searched as they leave the aircraft."

Real Barbershop Names

Grateful Heads
Barber Blacksheep
Herr Kutz
Talking Heads
Hackers
Hair on Earth

Hair Today, Gone
Tomorrow
Chop Shop
Hair Raisers
Get Buzzed
It'll Grow Back

@albz

There's no place like home. Unless you're a bee, in which case home is a terrible place filled with bees.

Strange English Subtitles from Hong Kong Martial Arts Movies

"Get out, you smurk!"
"Don't you feel the stink smell?"
"She's terrific. I can't stand her."
"You daring lousy guy."
"And you thought. I'm gabby bag."
"Suddenly my worm are all healed off."

Lunch Box Note Written By Parent
"New Rule: I will keep packing this sandwich until you eat it.
Good luck.
Love, Dad"

Real Petitions Filed with the Federal Government

- "Change the national anthem to R. Kelly's 2003 hit 'Ignition (Remix)'"
- "Convert at least one National Park into a dinosaur clone park"
- "Establish new legal system of motorcycle riding 'judges' who serve as police, judge, jury, and executioner all in one"
- "Join America and Australia to form Ameristralia"

Everything is funny, as long as it's happening to somebody else.

—Will Rogers

Names of Actual Boats

- *The Codfather*
- *Aqua Holic*
- *Vitamin Sea*
- *Marlin Monroe*
- *Duck Sloop*
- *Yacht to be Working*
- *Maid of Plywood*
- *Fah Get a Boat It*
- *My Widdle Wifeboat*
- *Costa Lotta*
- *Piece of Ship*

From a real court transcript:

Q: Do you know if your daughter has ever been involved in the voodoo or occult?

A: We both do.

Q: Voodoo?

A: We do.

Q: You do?

A: Yes, voodoo.

(B)Ad Campaign
Taking the "Got Milk?" campaign to Mexico, the Dairy Association translated its slogan into Spanish. Unfortunately, it came out as "Are you lactating?"

Sign on a road in Massachusetts:
"Entrance Only Do Not Enter"

Real Titles of Published Books
- Goblinproofing One's Chicken Coop
- How to Land a Top-Paying Pierogi Makers Job
- The Radiation Recipe Book
- Castration: The Advantages and the Disadvantages
- My Cat's in Love, or How to Survive Your Feline's Sex Life, Pregnancy, and Kittening
- Reusing Old Graves

What Some Hollywood Movies Were Called Overseas

- In Israel, *Cloudy with a Chance of Meatballs* was called *Rain of Falafel*.

- In Malaysia, *Austin Powers: The Spy Who Shagged Me* became *Austin Powers: The Spy Who Behaved Very Nicely Around Me*.

- In China, *Pretty Woman* was called *I Will Marry a Prostitute to Save Money*.

- In Germany, *Airplane!* was called *The Unbelievable Journey in a Crazy Airplane*.

- In China, *The Sixth Sense* was called *He's a Ghost!*

More Real Court Case Names

Schmuck v. United States

United States v. Ninety-five Barrels (More or Less) Alleged Apple Cider Vinegar

South Dakota v. Fifteen Impounded Cats

United States v. 11 1/4 Dozen Packages of Articles Labeled in Part Mrs. Moffat's Shoo-Fly Powders for Drunkenness

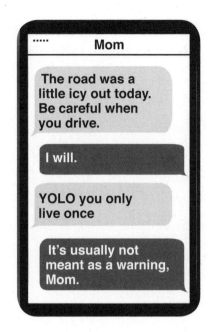

From a real court transcript:

Q: What is your date of birth?
A: July fifteenth.
Q: What year?
A: Every year.

***

Sign on restaurant door:
"We love kids, but please keep them at your table. Unattended kids will be given a shot of espresso and a free puppy."

The Worst Coffee Cup Name Misspellings

Shat (Chad)
Aiyon (Ian)
Hosee (Lucy)
Gimli (Emily)
Tsach (Zach)
Missle (Michelle)

More Accidentally Funny Headlines

Two Sisters Reunited After 18 Years at Checkout Counter

UTAH GIRL DOES WELL IN DOG SHOWS

Cuts Could Hurt Animals

TUNA BITING OFF WASHINGTON COAST

Safety Experts Say School Bus Passengers Should Be Belted

DEALERS WILL HEAR CAR TALK AT NOON

Dirty-Sounding Road Names
Booger Branch Road (Crandall, GA)
Butts Wynd Street (St. Andrews, Scotland)
Crotch Crescent (Oxfordshire, England)
Pe'e Pe'e Place (Hilo, HI)
Weiner Cutoff Road (Harrisburg, AK)
Spanker Lane (Derbyshire, England)
Butt Hollow Road (Salem, VA)

(B)Ad Campaign
The Big Mac was originally sold in France under the name *Gras Mec.* The expression means "big pimp" in French.

More Law Firm Names
Slappey & Sadd (Georgia)
Slaughter & Slaughter (California)
Sexter & Warmflash (New York)
Tittsworth & Grabbe (Georgia)
Walkup & Downing (California)
Rush, Rush & DeLay (Arkansas)

An ad displayed in shopping malls for
Creative Kids Software:
"So Fun, They Won't Even Know
Their Learning."

Inadvertently Naughty Newspaper Headlines

TREES CAN BREAK WIND

*Astronomers See Colorful Gas Clouds
Bubble Out of Uranus*

Butte Blast Blamed on Leaking Gas

CHILD'S STOOL GREAT FOR USE IN GARDEN

Body search reveals $4,000 in crack

**California Governor Makes Stand on
Dirty Toilets**

Tight end retires after colon surgery

_____

From a real court transcript:

Q: Doctor, will you take a look at those X-rays
and tell us something about the injury?

A: Let's see, which side am I testifying for?

Sign at a car dealership:
"The best way to get back on your feet—
miss a car payment."

More Couple Names from Wedding Announcements

Elizabeth MacDonald + Joel Berger =
MacDonald-Berger

Edna Gowen + Jason Getter = Gowen-Getter

Joe Looney + Shelby Warde = Looney-Warde

William Best + Jennifer Lay = Best-Lay

Daniel Hardy + Rachel Harr = Hardy-Harr

Amy Moore + Anthony Bacon = Moore-Bacon

Marissa Sawyer + Robert Hiney =
Sawyer-Hiney

Real Thank-You Note from a Kid
"Thank you mom for being wonderful, caring
& not making your meatloaf anymore"

From a real court transcript:

Q: Do you have any suggestions as to what prevented this from being a murder trial instead of an attempted-murder trial?

A: The victim lived.

> *Insanity runs in my family.*
> *It practically gallops.*
> —Cary Grant

(B)Ad Campaign
When the Sumitomo Corporation in Japan developed a strong steel pipe, it hired a Japanese advertising agency to market it in the United States. Big mistake: The agency named the pipe Sumitomo High Toughness, and launched a magazine ad campaign using the product's initials—SHT—in catchy slogans like "SHT-from Sumitomo" and "Now, Sumitomo brings SHT to the United States." Each ad ended with the assurance that SHT "was made to match its name."

License
to Chill

Driving
Miss Lazy

Unsinkable II

Sails Call
Apocalypso
Aloan Again
Pier Pressure
Seas the Day
Breakin' Wind
She Got the House
Dijabringbeeralong
Your Place Oar Mine

More Names of Actual Boats

John Barge's 2014 campaign for governor got off to a bad start. The front page of his official website said "John Barge: Georgia's Next Govenor." Barge, a former teacher, was the Georgia state school superintendent. (He lost.)

More Real Petitions Filed with the Federal Government
- "Make Batman Secretary of Defense"
- "Repeal the Second Law of Thermodynamics for a more perfect heat transfer"
- "Give everyone a unicorn and a lollipop for Boxing Day"
- "Allow the state of Canada to withdraw from the United States of America and create its own new government"
- "Nuke everything"

From a real court transcript:
Judge: I know you, don't I?
Defendant: Uh, yes.
Judge: Alright, how do I know you?
Defendant: Judge, do I have to tell you?
Judge: Of course, you might be obstructing justice not to tell me.
Defendant: Okay. I was your bookie.

Sign in an office:
"Would the person who took the step ladder yesterday please bring it back or further steps will be taken."

_____

A real call to tech support:
Caller: My computer has locked up, and no matter how many times I type "eleven," it won't unfreeze.
Tech: What do you mean, "type eleven"?
Caller: The message on my screen says, "Error Type 11."

_____

More Messages Seen on Church Reader Boards

"Blessing of pets. Bring your dog or cat or whatever and lawnchair."

"Whoever is praying for snow, please stop."

"He who farts in church sits in own pew."

"Don't let worries kill you. Let the church help."

"Get behind me, Satin."

"Whoever stole our AC units keep one; it is hot where you're going."

More English Subtitles from Hong Kong Martial Arts Movies

"You're a bad guy, where's your library card?"

"How can you use my intestines as a gift?"

"Check if there's a hole in my underpants."

"No! I saw a vomiting crab."

"You're stain!"

"Noodles? Forget it. Try my fist."

Nothing in life is fun for the whole family. There are no massage parlors with ice cream and free jewelry.

—Jerry Seinfeld

Actual Personalized License Plates

LOL OIL (on an electric car)

LOL MPG (on a gas guzzler)

RUBIX (on a Nissan Cube)

EWWWABUG (on a VW Beetle)

CRAMPED (on a Mini Cooper)

NOTDUMB (on a Smart Car)

Real Browser Extensions You Can Use While Surfing the Web

nCage: It replaces all images with ones of Nicolas Cage.

Millennials Begone: It replaces all instances of the word "millennials" with "pesky whipper-snappers."

Mustachio: It adds a huge, cartoonish handlebar  mustache to the faces of every photo.

Upside-Down: It makes everything upside-down.

In France, Cap'n Crunch is marketed under the name "Capitaine Crounche."

In 2006, Michigan election officials printed 180,000 mail-in ballots, and mailed out 10,000 of them before anyone noticed that they used the word *pubic* instead of *public*. (The remaining 170,000 ballots were reprinted at taxpayers' expense. Total cost: $40,000.)

Accidentally Funny Legal Headlines

Ten Commandments: Supreme Court Says
Some OK, Some Not

Doctor Testifies in Horse Suit

SILENT TEAMSTER GETS CRUEL
PUNISHMENT: LAWYER

Judges Appear More Lenient
on Crack Cocaine

LAWYERS GIVE POOR FREE LEGAL ADVICE

@badbanana

Can anyone recommend a few thousand
books on hoarding?

More Real Titles of Published Books
- *The Sunny Side of Bereavement*
- *Managing a Dental Practice: The Genghis Khan Way*
- *Hand Grenade Throwing as a College Sport*
- *Ghosts: Minnesota's Unnatural Resource*
- *Eating People Is Wrong*

Real Thank-You Note from a Kid
"Thank you mom for making me food so
I don't die"

More Quips from Flight Attendants

- "The yellow button above your head is the reading light; the orange button releases the hounds."

- "Sit back and relax, or lean forward all twisted up; the choice is yours."

- "Ladies and gentlemen, we will be turning down the cabin lights. This is for your comfort and to enhance the appearance of your flight attendants."

- "Please remain in your seats until Captain Crash and the crew have brought the aircraft to a screeching halt up against the gate. And once the tire smoke has cleared and the warning bells are silenced, we'll open the door and you can pick your way through the wreckage to the terminal."

Sign outside a new town hall:
"The town hall is closed until opening.
It will remain closed after being opened.
Open tomorrow."

More Passive-Aggressive Office Notes… and Responses

Please remember to date the food cans! Thanks!

Tried on 3 occasions to date cans. They only think of me as a friend…

DO NOT USE BUT ONE MICROWAVE AT A TIME. USING BOTH WILL TRIP FUSE AND NEITHER WILL WORK

Why are there two?

PLEASE KEEP THE DOOR CLOSED!!! THANK YOU!!!

Please don't use Comic Sans — we are a Fortune 500 company, not a lemonade stand.

More Real Road Names

This Street, That Street, and The Other Street
(three streets in Porters Lake, Nova Scotia)

Rue du Hâ Hâ (Chéroy, France)

Awesome Street (Cary, NC)

Farfrompoopen Road (only road to
Constipation Ridge in Story, AR)

From a real court transcript:
The Court: You've been charged with armed robbery. Do you want the court to appoint a lawyer to represent you?
Defendant: You don't have to appoint a very good lawyer, I'm going to plead guilty.

More of Robin's Outbursts from the '60s *Batman* TV Show

"Holy waste of energy, Batman!"

"Holy understatements, Batman!"

"Holy jelly molds, Batman!"

"Holy known unknown flying objects, Batman!"

"Holy bunions, Batman!"

"Holy astringent plumlike fruit, Batman!"

More Accidentally Funny Headlines

*Lawmakers Disagree Over Why
They Can't Agree*

**Most Doctors Agree Breathing Regularly
Is Good for You**

MAN SOUGHT FOR LEWD ACT

Man Steals Clock, Faces Time

ELIZABETH DOLE HAD NO CHOICE
BUT TO RUN AS A WOMAN

Mayor Parris to Homeless: Go Home

State Population to Double by 2040;
Babies to Blame

Woman Not Injured By Cookie

RALLY AGAINST APATHY DRAWS SMALL CROWD

Sign outside a London disco:
"Smarts is the most exclusive disco in town.
Everyone welcome."

When English/Spanish signs were first posted at Sky Harbor International Airport in Phoenix, they were full of translation mistakes. One sign to remind arriving travelers to declare produce and meats read *"Violadores Seran Finados,"* which translates as "Violators Will Be Deceased."

More Messages Seen on Church Reader Boards

"To err is human, to arrrr is pirate."

"The class on prophecy has been cancelled due to unforeseen circumstances."

"Forbidden fruit creates many jams"

"Pessimists need a kick in the can'ts"

"Bored? Try a missionary position."

"God didn't create anything without a purpose. But mosquitoes come close."

More Looney Laws

- Eating soup with a fork is against the law in New York.

- It's illegal to sell used confetti in Detroit.

- Men in Carmel, California, may not go out wearing an unmatching jacket and pants.

- In Connecticut, it's against the law to play Scrabble while waiting for a politician to speak.

(B)Ad Campaign
The Jotter is a brand of pen. It had to be renamed to be sold in some parts of Latin America, where *jotter* is slang for "jockstrap."

More Villages in the UK

Toad's Mouth	Shoot-up Hill
Lickey End	Slack Bottom
Maggots End	Pity Me
Crazies Hill	No Place
Bugs Bottom	World's End

Mom

Your great aunt just passed away. LOL.

Why is that funny?

Its not funny David! What do you mean?

Mom lol means laughing out loud!

Oh my goodness!! I sent that to everyone. I thought it meant lots of love. I have to call everyone back

WNDU, a local NBC affiliate in South Bend, Indiana, answered its own question when it displayed this on the screen: "School Two Easy For Kids?"

Lunch Box Note Written By Parent
"FYI: This was <u>NOT</u> made with love."

More Real Court Case Names

- *Terrible v. Terrible*
- *Nebraska v. One 1970 2-Door Sedan Rambler (Gremlin)*
- *United States v. Approximately 64,695 Pounds of Shark Fins*
- *United States v. Article Consisting of 50,000 Cardboard Boxes More or Less, Each Containing One Pair of Clacker Balls*
- *Juicy Whip v. Orange Bang*

@tazjordan

I just saw a sign outside of a bar on Sixth Street that said, "No smoking. No dogs. Definitely no smoking dogs."

Sign at pool:
"Welcome to our ool. Notice there is no 'P' in it. *Let's keep it that way."*

More English Subtitles from Hong Kong Martial Arts Movies

"You're bad. You make my busts up and down."

"He's Big Head Man, he is lousing around."

"You cheat ghosts to eat tofu?"

"D**n you, stink man!"

"Suck the coffin mushroom now."

"A big fool, with a gun, go to war. Surrendered and turned to a cake."

From a real court transcript:
Judge: You are charged with habitual drunkenness. Have you anything to say in your defense?
Defendant: Habitual thirstiness?

The French typing equivalent of "The quick brown fox jumped over the lazy dog" is "Take this old whiskey to the blonde judge who's smoking a cigar."

Dubious Menu Items Around the World
- Horse-rubbish sauce (Rome)
- Torture soup (Djerba, Tunisia)
- Terminal soup (Istanbul)
- Farte aux Fraises (Turkey)
- Frozen soap with Peccadilloes (Madrid)
- Stewed abalone with 3 things and lucky duck (Bangkok)

More Restaurant Names

Miso Hapi	Lord of the Fries
Custard's Last Stand	Lox, Stock and Bagel
Debbie Does Donuts	Just Falafs
Wok Around the Clock	Nin Com Soup

From a real court transcript:
Q: What happened then?
A: He says, "I have to kill you because you can identify me."
Q: Did he kill you?
A: No.

Real Roommate Notes...and Responses

These yogurts expired July 24. Today is Aug. 12. What should we do?

Run for our lives

PUT TOLIET SEAT DOWN

Spell toilet right

Do not use! I spit in this - since someone keeps using it. Thanks!

I spit in it too!

(B)Ad Campaign
GM cars were initially sold in Belgium using the slogan "Body by Fisher," which translated as "Corpse by Fisher."

Say it three times fast:
Geschwindigkeitsbegrenzung is German for "speed limit."

Celebrity Anagrams

Vin Diesel	I END LIVES
William Shatner	SLIM ALIEN WRATH
Howard Stern	TRASH WONDER
Alanis Morissette	IT'S NASAL, TIRESOME
Seinfeld	SNIDE ELF
Carly Simon	MOANS LYRIC
Carlos Santana	CARNAL SONATAS

Devil's Cigar
Gem-Studded Puffball
Trumpet of Death
Dead Man's Fingers

Velvet Foot
Witch's Butter
Octopus Stinkhorn
Bearded Tooth

Real Varieties of Mushrooms

More People's Names and Professions
Brad Slaughter, meat manager
Richard Frankenstein, doctor
Sam Sung, Apple specialist
Boot Shew, moonshiner
Alden Cockburn, urologist
Gregory Weed and Timothy Weed,
    brothers arrested for...weed.

@PaPaSkwat

I was in the grocery store. I saw a sign that said "pet supplies." So I did.

More Music Genres
Unblack Metal: Religious, god-worshiping metal music.
Mongolian Throat Singing Rap: It's exactly what it sounds like...

Real Bathroom Graffiti

Wanted – Telepath
(You know where to apply)

What if the hokey pokey really is what it's all about?

867-5309

AVOID LIFE.
IT'LL KILL YOU
IN THE END.

VU JA DE: The strange feeling that you've never been here before.

He who laughs last doesn't get the joke.

A proud new dad sits down to have a drink with his own father, who says:

"Son, now that you've got a kid of your own, I think it's time you had this."

"Dad, you don't mean…"

The older dad hands his son a copy of *Dad Jokes.*

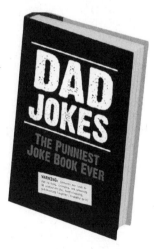

"Dad," the son says, tears welling up in the corners of his eyes. "I'm honored."

"Hi, honored," his father replies. "I'm Dad."

Image Credits